ROSICRUCIA

GW01402806

ESOTERIC TRADITION, PHILOSOPHY AND LEGACY OF THE ROSICRUCIAN ORDER

4 BOOKS IN 1

BOOK 1
THE ORIGINS OF ROSICRUCIAN MYSTICISM: SECRETS OF THE ANCIENT BROTHERHOOD

BOOK 2
ALCHEMY AND THE ROSICRUCIAN TRADITION: UNLOCKING THE HIDDEN SYMBOLS

BOOK 3
THE PHILOSOPHY OF THE ROSY CROSS: ENLIGHTENMENT AND INNER TRANSFORMATION

BOOK 4
ROSICRUCIANISM AND ITS INFLUENCE ON MODERN OCCULTISM

SAMUEL SHEPHERD

Published by Samuel Shepherd
Library of Congress Cataloging-in-Publication Data
ISBN 978-1-83938-872-9
Cover design by Rizzo

Disclaimer

The contents of this book are based on extensive research and the best available historical sources. However, the author and publisher make no claims, promises, or guarantees about the accuracy, completeness, or adequacy of the information contained herein. The information in this book is provided on an "as is" basis, and the author and publisher disclaim any and all liability for any errors, omissions, or inaccuracies in the information or for any actions taken in reliance on such information. The opinions and views expressed in this book are those of the author and do not necessarily reflect the official policy or position of any organization or individual mentioned in this book. Any reference to specific people, places, or events is intended only to provide historical context and is not intended to defame or malign any group, individual, or entity. The information in this book is intended for educational and entertainment purposes only. It is not intended to be a substitute for professional advice or judgment. Readers are encouraged to conduct their own research and to seek professional advice where appropriate. Every effort has been made to obtain necessary permissions and acknowledgments for all images and other copyrighted material used in this book. Any errors or omissions in this regard are unintentional, and the author and publisher will correct them in future editions.

BOOK 1 - THE ORIGINS OF ROSICRUCIAN MYSTICISM: SECRETS OF THE ANCIENT BROTHERHOOD

BOOK 2 - ALCHEMY AND THE ROSICRUCIAN TRADITION: UNLOCKING THE HIDDEN SYMBOLS

BOOK 3 - THE PHILOSOPHY OF THE ROSY CROSS: ENLIGHTENMENT AND INNER TRANSFORMATION

BOOK 4 - ROSICRUCIANISM AND ITS INFLUENCE ON MODERN OCCULTISM

Introduction

Rosicrucianism: Esoteric Tradition, Philosophy, and Legacy of the Rosicrucian Order is a comprehensive journey into the profound mysticism, symbolism, and philosophy of one of the most enigmatic spiritual traditions in Western esotericism. For centuries, the Rosicrucian Order has captivated seekers of truth, wisdom, and enlightenment, drawing them into a world of alchemical transformation, hidden knowledge, and philosophical insight. This collection of four volumes offers a thorough exploration of the origins, teachings, and lasting influence of the Rosicrucian tradition, illuminating the path toward self-realization and spiritual mastery.

Book 1, *The Origins of Rosicrucian Mysticism: Secrets of the Ancient Brotherhood*, takes readers into the heart of the mysterious origins of Rosicrucianism. It uncovers the early foundations of this secretive brotherhood, revealing its links to Gnosticism, Hermeticism, and the occult knowledge passed down through hidden schools of mysticism. Through the exploration of the early Rosicrucian manifestos and the spiritual ideals that shaped the order, readers will discover the ancient roots of this esoteric tradition and the ways in which it has been guarded and preserved over the centuries.

Book 2, *Alchemy and the Rosicrucian Tradition: Unlocking the Hidden Symbols*, delves into the deeply symbolic world of alchemy, a central element of Rosicrucian practice. The book examines the alchemical process as both a physical and spiritual transformation, decoding the hidden meanings behind symbols like the Philosopher's Stone, the elements, and the stages of purification. By understanding the significance of alchemical symbolism within Rosicrucianism, readers will gain insights into the path of inner transformation that has guided countless seekers toward enlightenment.

In Book 3, *The Philosophy of the Rosy Cross: Enlightenment and Inner Transformation*, the deeper philosophical aspects of Rosicrucianism are explored, particularly its focus on personal mastery and the realization of the higher self. Through the lens of the Rosy Cross, a powerful symbol representing the union of opposites—spirit and matter, life and death—this volume guides readers through the profound inner alchemical journey that leads to spiritual awakening and the harmonization of the individual with the cosmic order.

Book 4, *Rosicrucianism and Its Influence on Modern Occultism*, demonstrates the enduring legacy of Rosicrucian thought in contemporary spiritual movements and occult traditions. From the Hermetic Order of the Golden Dawn to modern mystical practices, Rosicrucianism has profoundly shaped the way esoteric traditions have evolved in the modern era. This book examines the ways in which the symbols, rituals, and philosophies of Rosicrucianism continue to influence occult practices, magical orders, and even New Age spirituality, revealing how this timeless tradition remains relevant and transformative today.

This bundle is designed to serve as both an introduction and an in-depth exploration of Rosicrucianism's rich legacy, offering readers a pathway into the hidden wisdom of this mystical tradition. Whether you are new to esoteric studies or a seasoned seeker, *Rosicrucianism: Esoteric Tradition, Philosophy, and Legacy of the Rosicrucian Order* provides a gateway to the profound teachings, symbolic practices, and spiritual mysteries that have inspired generations of initiates. Through these four volumes, you will embark on a transformative journey, guided by the ancient wisdom of the Rosicrucian Order, toward deeper understanding and personal enlightenment.

BOOK 1
THE ORIGINS OF ROSICRUCIAN MYSTICISM
SECRETS OF THE ANCIENT BROTHERHOOD
SAMUEL SHEPHERD

Chapter 1: The Mysterious Beginnings: Tracing the Rosicrucian Lineage

The origins of Rosicrucianism are shrouded in mystery, blending legend, historical speculation, and esoteric symbolism. The Rosicrucian tradition is said to have emerged during the early 17th century with the publication of the three manifestos: *Fama Fraternitatis*, *Confessio Fraternitatis*, and *The Chymical Wedding of Christian Rosenkreuz*. These works spoke of a secret brotherhood dedicated to the pursuit of knowledge, spiritual enlightenment, and the reformation of society. Central to this narrative is the figure of Christian Rosenkreuz, a semi-mythical founder whose life and journey encapsulate the essence of Rosicrucianism. While the manifestos describe the mission of the brotherhood, the lineage of Rosicrucianism stretches further back, drawing from diverse traditions of mysticism, alchemy, and esoteric philosophy.

Christian Rosenkreuz, according to the *Fama Fraternitatis*, was a German nobleman born in the late 14th century. He is said to have embarked on a pilgrimage through the Middle East, where he studied with sages and alchemists, absorbing ancient wisdom from the Arabic, Jewish, and Christian mystical traditions. After years of learning, he returned to Europe with the intention of sharing the knowledge he had gathered. It was in this context that the brotherhood of the Rosy Cross was established, a secretive group of learned men who sought to reform science, religion, and society. However, the brotherhood chose to remain hidden, disseminating their teachings through cryptic symbols, allegories, and the publication of their manifestos.

Though Christian Rosenkreuz's existence remains debated by scholars, many believe that his story is symbolic rather than historical. The account of his travels and the founding of the brotherhood serves as a metaphor for the spiritual journey of enlightenment, a path marked by personal transformation and the pursuit of esoteric truths. His name itself, "Rosenkreuz," which translates to "Rose Cross," is rich in symbolism. The rose, often associated with beauty, secrecy, and regeneration, combined with the cross, a symbol of suffering, death, and resurrection, reflects the union of opposites in alchemy and mysticism—a core theme in Rosicrucian thought.

Tracing the lineage of Rosicrucianism reveals deep connections with earlier traditions of mysticism, particularly those rooted in the Hermetic and alchemical schools. Hermeticism, which emerged from ancient Egypt and Greece, emphasized the interconnectedness of all things in the universe, teaching that the microcosm and macrocosm reflect each other. This principle, known as "as above, so below," became central to Rosicrucian thought, where the processes of alchemy and personal spiritual development mirrored the transformations occurring in the natural world. Hermetic writings such as the *Emerald Tablet* profoundly influenced the Rosicrucian worldview, emphasizing the importance of inner knowledge, spiritual purification, and the transmutation of the soul.

Alchemy itself played a significant role in the Rosicrucian tradition. The alchemists' search for the Philosopher's Stone—the substance capable of turning base metals into gold—was more than a physical pursuit. It was symbolic of the spiritual quest to achieve inner enlightenment and transformation. The Rosicrucians adopted these alchemical principles, emphasizing that true wisdom and power came from within, through the purification of the soul and the alignment with divine principles. Their manifestos, particularly *The Chymical Wedding of Christian Rosenkreuz*, are filled with alchemical symbolism, portraying a journey of inner transformation through allegory.

The roots of Rosicrucianism also intertwine with the Gnostic tradition, which emerged during the early centuries of Christianity. Gnosticism emphasized the acquisition of secret knowledge (gnosis) as the path to spiritual salvation. For Gnostics, the material world was a prison from which the soul needed to escape through enlightenment. This theme resonated with the Rosicrucians, who viewed the world as a place of spiritual darkness, in need of reformation through the light of hidden wisdom. Like the Gnostics, the

Rosicrucians believed that this knowledge was not accessible to all, but only to those initiated into the mysteries of the brotherhood.

Another key influence on Rosicrucianism was the Kabbalah, the Jewish mystical tradition that interprets the Torah through layers of symbolic meaning. Kabbalistic teachings, particularly regarding the nature of the divine, the structure of the universe, and the process of spiritual ascent, found their way into Rosicrucian doctrine. The Kabbalistic Tree of Life, a diagram that represents the journey of the soul towards unity with the divine, parallels the Rosicrucian view of spiritual progression. The Rosicrucians, like the Kabbalists, sought to understand the hidden forces that govern the universe and to use that knowledge to transcend the limitations of human existence.

In exploring the mysterious beginnings of Rosicrucianism, it is impossible to ignore the influence of the Renaissance, a period marked by the revival of ancient wisdom and the pursuit of universal knowledge. The intellectual environment of Renaissance Europe, with its emphasis on the rediscovery of classical texts and the synthesis of science, religion, and philosophy, created fertile ground for the emergence of esoteric traditions like Rosicrucianism. The spread of Hermeticism, alchemy, and Kabbalah during this period provided the foundation upon which the Rosicrucian tradition was built.

Chapter 2: The Fama Fraternitatis: The First Manifesto of the Brotherhood

The *Fama Fraternitatis*, or the "Fame of the Brotherhood," is considered the first manifesto of the Rosicrucian Order and serves as a cornerstone for understanding the ideals and mission of this secretive group. Published anonymously in 1614, it introduces the world to the existence of the Fraternity of the Rosy Cross, a mystical brotherhood with the goal of reforming science, religion, and society. The *Fama* is written in a narrative form and recounts the life and work of Christian Rosenkreuz, the legendary founder of the Rosicrucian Order, while also outlining the purposes and ideals of the brotherhood. At its heart, the *Fama* is both a call to the enlightened minds of Europe and a critique of the state of knowledge and spiritual understanding at the time.

The manifesto opens with an account of the early life of Christian Rosenkreuz, who is described as a nobleman born in Germany in the late 14th century. He is portrayed as an extraordinary individual who embarked on a pilgrimage to the Middle East in search of wisdom. During his travels, Rosenkreuz is said to have studied under various masters in places like Damascus and Fez, where he was initiated into ancient esoteric knowledge. He learned alchemy, natural philosophy, and mystical teachings, which he later sought to share with the Western world. Upon returning to Europe, Rosenkreuz found that the knowledge he had acquired was either misunderstood or ignored, so he decided to establish a secret brotherhood—the Rosicrucians—dedicated to preserving and disseminating this wisdom.

The *Fama Fraternitatis* presents Christian Rosenkreuz not only as a seeker of knowledge but also as a reformer. His intent was to bring about a transformation of society through the application of spiritual and scientific knowledge. The manifesto critiques the existing institutions of the time, particularly the Catholic Church and the universities, accusing them of failing to promote true knowledge and enlightenment. In this sense, the *Fama* can be seen as a revolutionary document, advocating for a new way of thinking that blends the spiritual with the rational. It calls for a return to the study of nature and divine law, in opposition to the dogma and superstition that, according to the Rosicrucians, dominated the religious and scientific institutions of the time.

One of the most intriguing aspects of the *Fama Fraternitatis* is its emphasis on secrecy. The brotherhood is described as invisible, with members working in anonymity for the betterment of society. They are not to seek personal fame or recognition, and their work is to remain hidden from the uninitiated. This secrecy is central to the Rosicrucian tradition, reflecting the belief that true wisdom is reserved for those who are spiritually prepared to receive it. The *Fama* also insists that the brotherhood does not seek material wealth or power, distancing itself from political or economic ambitions. Instead, the Rosicrucians aim to live in harmony with nature and to use their knowledge to serve humanity.

The manifesto also contains a fascinating allegory of the discovery of Christian Rosenkreuz's tomb, which is said to have occurred 120 years after his death. The tomb, described as a seven-sided vault, is filled with symbolic items, including alchemical instruments and esoteric writings. The discovery of this tomb is presented as a pivotal moment in the history of the brotherhood, marking the reawakening of its mission after a long period of dormancy. The vault itself is rich in symbolic meaning, representing not only the physical resting place of Rosenkreuz but also the repository of the hidden knowledge that the Rosicrucians possess. The tomb's discovery is framed as an invitation to those who are worthy to join the brotherhood in its mission to transform society.

In addition to its critique of society and institutions, the *Fama Fraternitatis* outlines the principles that guide the Rosicrucian Order. These principles emphasize the importance of harmony with nature, the pursuit of spiritual wisdom, and the practice of altruism. The brotherhood seeks to heal both individuals and society, using their esoteric knowledge for the common good. The manifesto also emphasizes the interconnectedness of all things, reflecting the Hermetic belief that the microcosm reflects the macrocosm. This philosophical perspective, which draws on Hermeticism, alchemy, and other esoteric traditions, is foundational to the Rosicrucian worldview.

The *Fama* sparked a great deal of interest and controversy upon its publication. Some readers saw it as a genuine call to join a hidden brotherhood, while others dismissed it as a hoax or a satire. Regardless of its factual basis, the manifesto had a profound impact on European intellectual and occult circles. It was quickly followed by the publication of two other Rosicrucian manifestos: the *Confessio Fraternitatis* in 1615 and *The Chymical Wedding of Christian Rosenkreuz* in 1617. Together, these texts form the core of the Rosicrucian literary tradition, outlining the goals, beliefs, and methods of the brotherhood.

The response to the *Fama* was immediate and widespread. Across Europe, intellectuals, alchemists, and mystics debated its contents and the existence of the Rosicrucian Order. Some were inspired to join what they believed to be a real movement for spiritual and scientific reform, while others were skeptical. The mysterious nature of the brotherhood, coupled with the symbolic richness of the *Fama*, made it a compelling document for those interested in the occult and esoteric traditions. Its influence extended far beyond its initial publication, contributing to the development of later esoteric movements, including Freemasonry, Theosophy, and the Hermetic Order of the Golden Dawn.

The *Fama Fraternitatis* also reflects the broader intellectual and spiritual currents of its time. The early 17th century was a period of great upheaval and transformation in Europe, marked by the rise of scientific inquiry, religious conflict, and the search for new philosophical frameworks. The Rosicrucian manifesto tapped into the desire for a new synthesis of knowledge that could reconcile science, religion, and mysticism. In this sense, the *Fama* can be seen as a product of the Renaissance and the early modern period, reflecting the aspirations and anxieties of a world in transition.

Chapter 3: Christian Rosenkreuz: The Myth and Legend

Christian Rosenkreuz stands as one of the most enigmatic figures in Western esoteric traditions, his name and story entwined with the foundations of Rosicrucianism. He is depicted as the founder of the Rosicrucian Order, a secretive brotherhood devoted to the pursuit of knowledge, spiritual enlightenment, and the reformation of society. Yet, the figure of Rosenkreuz is wrapped in layers of myth, allegory, and symbolism, leading to widespread debate about whether he was a real historical person or a purely symbolic creation. The legend of Christian Rosenkreuz is a tale of mystery, travel, hidden wisdom, and the transformative power of esoteric knowledge.

According to the Rosicrucian manifestos, particularly the *Fama Fraternitatis*, Christian Rosenkreuz was born in 1378 to a noble family in Germany. His early years are marked by an insatiable thirst for knowledge. At a young age, he set out on a journey to the East in search of wisdom, a pilgrimage that would form the foundation of his later spiritual teachings. Rosenkreuz's travels took him to the Middle East, where he studied with sages, mystics, and alchemists in countries like Arabia, Egypt, and possibly even Persia. During these years, he is said to have gained profound knowledge of the natural world, the divine mysteries, and the workings of the universe, absorbing teachings from Islamic, Jewish, and Christian esoteric traditions.

His journey can be interpreted not only as a physical expedition but also as a metaphor for the spiritual path. In many mystical traditions, the "East" represents a place of spiritual awakening and wisdom, and Rosenkreuz's travels serve as a symbolic journey into the heart of esoteric knowledge. The account of his pilgrimage mirrors the alchemical process, in which an individual undergoes stages of transformation in the pursuit of enlightenment. In this context, Rosenkreuz's travels represent the stages of personal purification and spiritual refinement, necessary to achieve a higher understanding of divine truths.

Upon his return to Europe, Christian Rosenkreuz found himself disillusioned with the state of knowledge and spirituality in the West. The existing institutions, particularly the universities and the Church, were entrenched in dogma and resistant to the kinds of enlightened teachings he had encountered in the East. Recognizing the need for a profound transformation in the understanding of science, religion, and society, Rosenkreuz resolved to establish a secret fraternity, the Rosicrucians, which would work in silence to bring about this reformation. This brotherhood would share the wisdom of the ancients, but only with those deemed spiritually prepared to receive it.

The creation of the Rosicrucian Order marks a pivotal moment in the legend of Christian Rosenkreuz. He and his followers, according to the *Fama Fraternitatis*, sought to live in harmony with nature, free from personal ambition and dedicated to the service of humanity. They chose to remain hidden from the world, carrying out their work in secret, which only added to the mystery surrounding their existence. The brotherhood, under Rosenkreuz's guidance, rejected materialism and the pursuit of personal fame or wealth, instead focusing on spiritual knowledge, the healing of the sick, and the upliftment of society.

One of the central episodes in the legend of Christian Rosenkreuz is the discovery of his tomb, as described in the *Fama Fraternitatis*. The tomb, said to be found 120 years after his death, is portrayed as a mystical, seven-sided vault, filled with alchemical symbols and esoteric writings. Inside the tomb, the body of Rosenkreuz is discovered, perfectly preserved, as though in a state of suspended animation. This discovery is more than a historical event within the narrative; it is an allegory of the timeless nature of spiritual wisdom. The preservation of Rosenkreuz's body represents the undying truth of the Rosicrucian teachings, which were not meant for the masses but reserved for those who could understand and apply them in their own spiritual lives.

The symbolism of the rose and the cross, which form the basis of Rosenkreuz's name, is integral to understanding his legend. The rose, a symbol of beauty, mystery, and spiritual unfoldment, combined with the cross, a representation of suffering, death, and resurrection, embodies the alchemical and mystical philosophy of the Rosicrucians. The union of these two symbols reflects the process of inner transformation that lies at the heart of the Rosicrucian path: the idea that one must endure trials and suffering to achieve spiritual rebirth and enlightenment. This theme is consistent throughout the Rosicrucian writings and serves as a metaphor for the alchemical process of turning base materials into gold, symbolizing the transmutation of the soul.

The figure of Christian Rosenkreuz has sparked significant debate and speculation among scholars, occultists, and historians. Some have argued that he is purely a mythical or allegorical figure, created by the authors of the Rosicrucian manifestos to represent the ideals of the brotherhood.

Others have attempted to identify him with historical individuals, though no definitive evidence has been found to support these claims. Regardless of whether Rosenkreuz was a real person or a symbolic construct, his story has had a profound influence on the development of Western esoteric thought. The ideals of Christian Rosenkreuz—personal transformation, spiritual enlightenment, and the pursuit of hidden knowledge—have echoed throughout centuries of occult traditions, shaping movements such as Freemasonry, Theosophy, and the Hermetic Order of the Golden Dawn.

The legend of Christian Rosenkreuz continues to capture the imagination of those interested in the mysteries of the Rosicrucians. His story, filled with elements of mysticism, alchemy, and spiritual journeying, serves as both a reflection of the broader esoteric traditions that preceded Rosicrucianism and as a blueprint for the inner path of enlightenment that the brotherhood promoted. As the mythical founder of the Rosicrucians, Christian Rosenkreuz stands as a symbol of the transformative power of hidden wisdom and the eternal quest for spiritual knowledge.

Chapter 4: The Invisible College: Origins of the Hidden Mystics

The concept of the Invisible College is integral to the history and mystique of Rosicrucianism, often serving as a bridge between the hidden knowledge of the past and the intellectual and spiritual movements that followed. While its origins are steeped in secrecy, the Invisible College is commonly described as an informal network of thinkers, mystics, and scholars who operated outside the confines of established academic institutions and religious dogmas. These individuals sought to pursue deeper truths through a combination of scientific inquiry, mystical contemplation, and esoteric knowledge. Though not a formalized organization, the Invisible College represented a gathering of enlightened minds who aimed to reform not only science and philosophy but also society itself.

The notion of an Invisible College reflects the Rosicrucian ideal of an underground brotherhood of intellectuals and mystics, united by their desire to understand the hidden forces of the universe. This network of individuals, working behind the scenes, was said to share secret knowledge, especially in the fields of alchemy, natural philosophy, and metaphysical spirituality. Their collaboration was based on a profound belief that divine truths could be accessed not only through religious faith but through the study of nature, science, and inner spiritual development. These secret exchanges of ideas are thought to have laid the groundwork for many of the later developments in both the scientific revolution and the esoteric traditions that shaped modern occultism.

The origins of the Invisible College can be traced to the Renaissance period, a time when the rediscovery of classical knowledge and the rise of humanist philosophy fostered a renewed interest in ancient wisdom. During this era, European intellectuals became increasingly dissatisfied with the rigid teachings of the Church and the scholastic institutions of the time, which were seen as out of touch with new discoveries in science and metaphysics. Renaissance humanism, with its emphasis on individual inquiry and the study of ancient texts, opened the door to a broader exploration of the natural world, often leading to the blending of scientific and mystical thought. It was within this climate that the idea of a secretive group of enlightened individuals began to take shape.

Many of those who are believed to have been part of the Invisible College were inspired by the works of earlier mystical and alchemical traditions, such as Hermeticism, Gnosticism, and Kabbalah. These traditions emphasized the unity of the divine and natural worlds, teaching that hidden truths could be found within both the macrocosm of the universe and the microcosm of the human soul. Hermetic texts like the *Emerald Tablet* and the writings attributed to Hermes Trismegistus became central to the beliefs of these hidden scholars, who saw in them a roadmap to divine wisdom. The Invisible College drew on this ancient esoteric knowledge while also embracing new scientific methods that were emerging during the period.

One of the most notable aspects of the Invisible College was its rejection of public recognition and its preference for anonymity. The very name "Invisible College" emphasizes the group's clandestine nature. Unlike formal universities or religious institutions, the members of the Invisible College did not seek to establish a school or public platform. Instead, they operated through private correspondence, secret meetings, and coded writings that only the initiated could understand. This hidden structure allowed them to pursue their studies free from the interference of the authorities, who often regarded their activities as heretical or dangerous. Their decision to remain invisible also reflected a deeper spiritual philosophy: true wisdom, they believed, was not for the masses but for those who were spiritually prepared to receive it.

The Invisible College played a pivotal role in the development of early modern science. Many of its members were deeply involved in the study of alchemy, which at the time was not just concerned with the transmutation of metals but with the transformation of the soul. These alchemical principles—where material change was seen as a reflection of inner spiritual evolution—dovetailed with the Rosicrucian ideal of personal enlightenment through the pursuit of hidden knowledge. The work of these early alchemists, mystics, and natural philosophers laid the groundwork for what would later become modern chemistry, physics, and astronomy.

One of the figures often associated with the Invisible College is Sir Francis Bacon, an influential philosopher and statesman of the early 17th century. Bacon's work, particularly his ideas on the scientific method and empirical inquiry, reflected many of the ideals associated with the Invisible College. Though not explicitly linked to the Rosicrucian manifestos, Bacon's vision of a utopian society dedicated to knowledge, as outlined in his work *The New Atlantis*, bears striking similarities to the Rosicrucian vision of a hidden brotherhood working for the betterment of humanity. Bacon's promotion of experimental science and his belief that nature could be understood through systematic investigation were key to the intellectual environment that nurtured the Invisible College.

The Invisible College is also thought to have influenced the foundation of the Royal Society of London in 1660, one of the earliest scientific societies in the modern sense. Many of the founding members of the Royal Society had ties to the mystical and alchemical traditions of the Invisible College, and they carried forward the group's commitment to the study of nature, the promotion of science, and the pursuit of hidden knowledge. Though the Royal Society became more focused on empirical science over time, its origins were deeply rooted in the same blend of mystical and scientific inquiry that had characterized the Invisible College.

The legacy of the Invisible College continued to shape esoteric and scientific thought long after its peak. Its influence can be seen in the growth of other secretive groups, such as the Freemasons and the Hermetic Order of the Golden Dawn, both of which emphasized the combination of mystical philosophy with the scientific and spiritual pursuit of enlightenment. The members of the Invisible College, while remaining hidden from public view, left an indelible mark on the intellectual history of Europe, fostering an environment where the boundaries between science, mysticism, and philosophy blurred, creating a space where new ideas could flourish outside the constraints of mainstream society.

Chapter 5: Hermeticism and Rosicrucian Thought: A Shared Esoteric Tradition

Hermeticism and Rosicrucianism share a deep and intertwined history, each contributing to a rich tapestry of esoteric thought that has shaped Western mysticism. At the heart of both traditions lies the belief in the interconnectedness of the universe, the microcosm and macrocosm, and the possibility of spiritual transformation through hidden knowledge. Hermeticism, which has its roots in the ancient writings attributed to Hermes Trismegistus, and Rosicrucianism, emerging in the early 17th century, share a profound commitment to the study of divine principles through both inner reflection and the natural world. The influence of Hermetic thought on the development of Rosicrucianism is undeniable, and the two traditions often overlap in their philosophical outlooks, symbolic language, and mystical objectives.

Hermeticism traces its origins to the Hermetic texts, especially the *Corpus Hermeticum* and the *Emerald Tablet*, which are believed to have been written between the first and third centuries AD. These texts convey a spiritual philosophy that emphasizes the unity of all things and the pursuit of gnosis, or divine knowledge. Hermes Trismegistus, the mythical figure from whom Hermeticism takes its name, is portrayed as a sage who bridges the human and divine realms, teaching the mysteries of the cosmos, the nature of the divine, and the path to spiritual enlightenment. Central to Hermetic philosophy is the idea that the material world is a reflection of the divine, and that through understanding the natural world, one can access higher spiritual truths.

The principle of "as above, so below" is perhaps the most famous Hermetic axiom, encapsulating the belief that the macrocosm (the universe) and the microcosm (the individual) are mirrors of each other. This concept became foundational not only to Hermeticism but also to Rosicrucian thought. In both traditions, the process of spiritual transformation is understood as an alchemical journey, where the individual seeks to purify their inner being in the same way that an alchemist might attempt to transmute base metals into gold. This spiritual alchemy is not simply a quest for material wealth or power but a profound metaphor for the elevation of the soul, an idea that resonates throughout the Rosicrucian manifestos.

Rosicrucianism, which emerged during the early 17th century with the publication of the *Fama Fraternitatis*, *Confessio Fraternitatis*, and *The Chymical Wedding of Christian Rosenkreuz*, owes much of its esoteric framework to Hermeticism. The Rosicrucian manifestos introduced the world to a secret brotherhood devoted to the reformation of science, religion, and society, using hidden wisdom derived from ancient traditions. The central figure of Rosicrucianism, Christian Rosenkreuz, is often depicted as a traveler who acquires secret knowledge in the East, much like the journey of the Hermetic seeker, who gains wisdom through study and spiritual practice. In both cases, the pursuit of divine knowledge is viewed as the key to understanding the universe and achieving personal transformation.

Hermetic teachings also shaped Rosicrucian symbolism, particularly in the realm of alchemy. The alchemical process, central to both Hermetic and Rosicrucian thought, is seen as a path to spiritual enlightenment rather than merely a quest to manipulate physical matter. The Rosicrucian writings are filled with alchemical imagery, using it as an allegory for the purification and perfection of the soul. The alchemical wedding, or the union of opposites, represents the integration of the masculine and feminine, the material and the spiritual, and is a theme that permeates both traditions. This synthesis of opposites reflects the Hermetic belief that all dualities, whether they be light and dark, body and spirit, or male and female, are ultimately expressions of a single divine source.

Another key shared concept between Hermeticism and Rosicrucianism is the idea of divine revelation through nature. Hermeticism teaches that the natural world is a reflection of the divine mind, and that by studying the patterns, cycles, and structures of nature, one can come to understand the will of God. This emphasis on the divine in nature is mirrored in Rosicrucianism, where the members of the brotherhood are often depicted as natural philosophers or scientists who use their knowledge of the natural world to unlock spiritual truths. The Rosicrucians, like the Hermeticists before them, believed that nature was not separate from the divine but was a manifestation of divine principles. This view influenced the development of natural philosophy during the Renaissance and the Enlightenment, where figures such as Isaac Newton and Robert Fludd drew upon both Hermetic and Rosicrucian ideas in their scientific and mystical inquiries.

The esoteric tradition of Hermeticism also contributed to the Rosicrucian belief in the possibility of human divinization. In both traditions, the seeker is seen as a reflection of the divine, with the potential to transcend ordinary human limitations through spiritual practice and the acquisition of wisdom. Hermetic teachings emphasize the idea that humanity is inherently divine, but has become trapped in the material world and must seek to return to its divine origins through spiritual knowledge. This theme is echoed in Rosicrucianism, where the individual's journey toward enlightenment involves shedding the illusions of the material world and awakening to their divine potential. In both systems, the ultimate goal is to achieve a state of union with the divine, often depicted as the culmination of the alchemical or mystical process.

The connection between Hermeticism and Rosicrucianism also extends to their shared emphasis on initiation and secrecy. Both traditions viewed their teachings as sacred and intended for a select group of individuals who were spiritually prepared to receive them. The Rosicrucian brotherhood, like the Hermetic schools of thought, operated in secret, communicating through symbolic language and allegories that only the initiated could fully comprehend. This emphasis on secrecy reflects the belief that true wisdom is not for the masses, but for those who have undertaken the necessary spiritual preparation to understand and apply it. This exclusivity is a hallmark of both traditions, where initiation into the mysteries is seen as a rite of passage that marks the beginning of the seeker's journey toward enlightenment.

In both Hermeticism and Rosicrucianism, the pursuit of hidden knowledge is not an intellectual exercise alone but a transformative spiritual practice. The seeker in both traditions is encouraged to engage with the world through a combination of study, contemplation, and personal experience, with the aim of achieving a deeper understanding of the divine and their place within the cosmos.

Chapter 6: Alchemy and Divine Transformation: The Secret Teachings of the Rosy Cross

Alchemy, a central element in the teachings of the Rosy Cross, goes beyond the mere transmutation of metals into gold. For the Rosicrucians, alchemy is both a physical and spiritual process, symbolizing the transformation of the human soul from its base state into a perfected, enlightened being. This quest for divine transformation, often referred to as the "Great Work" or *Magnum Opus*, involves not only external experimentation but also an inward journey of purification and enlightenment. The secret teachings of the Rosy Cross emphasize that this alchemical process is, at its core, a deeply spiritual undertaking, where the transmutation of matter serves as a metaphor for the soul's evolution toward a state of unity with the divine.

In Rosicrucian thought, the practice of alchemy is understood to mirror the stages of personal spiritual development. The alchemical processes of calcination, dissolution, conjunction, and coagulation—stages involved in turning base matter into gold—are symbolic of the various stages a person undergoes on the path to spiritual enlightenment. Calcination, the first stage, represents the burning away of impurities and the destruction of the ego. In this process, the Rosicrucian adept must confront the baser aspects of their personality—pride, selfishness, and material attachment—in order to begin the process of spiritual refinement. This phase is often painful, as it involves a symbolic death of the ego, but it is essential for the transformation to take place.

Following the calcination phase, the alchemical process moves to dissolution, where the purified self begins to dissolve the boundaries between the individual and the spiritual forces of the universe. In Rosicrucian teachings, dissolution is the stage where the seeker's rigid perceptions of the world begin to melt away, allowing them to see beyond the illusions of the material world. This is not simply an intellectual exercise but a profound spiritual experience in which the individual starts to experience the interconnectedness of all things. In the Rosicrucian tradition, this phase is marked by deep meditation, reflection, and inner revelation, as the seeker gains insight into the divine order that underpins the universe.

Conjunction, the next phase in the alchemical process, symbolizes the union of opposites—the reconciliation of the spiritual and material, the masculine and feminine, the conscious and unconscious. In Rosicrucian alchemy, this phase is of profound importance because it represents the moment when the seeker integrates their higher, divine self with their earthly, material existence. The union of opposites reflects the idea that true enlightenment is not about escaping the material world but about finding harmony between the spiritual and physical planes. The Rosicrucian adept, having purified and dissolved their ego, now begins to rebuild their self, but in alignment with divine principles. This stage of conjunction represents a marriage of the spiritual and the material, leading to a more complete and balanced state of being.

The final stage in the alchemical process is coagulation, where the seeker achieves a state of permanence and stability in their new, transformed state. This is the culmination of the alchemical journey, where the perfected soul emerges, symbolized by the Philosopher's Stone, which has the power to transform base metals into gold. For the Rosicrucians, the Philosopher's Stone is not a physical object but a metaphor for the ultimate state of spiritual attainment—the divine wisdom and eternal life that comes with true enlightenment. Coagulation represents the final integration of the self, where the spiritual and physical are permanently united, and the seeker has achieved a state of divine awareness.

Throughout these stages, the teachings of the Rosy Cross emphasize that the alchemical process is not a solitary endeavor. The Rosicrucians believed that spiritual transformation required not only individual effort but also the guidance of hidden wisdom and the support of a like-minded brotherhood. The alchemical teachings of the Rosy Cross were often communicated through cryptic symbols, allegories, and rituals designed to guide the seeker on their spiritual path. This secrecy was not meant to exclude but to ensure that only those who were truly prepared and spiritually mature could understand and benefit from the teachings. The Rosicrucians recognized that true wisdom could be dangerous if misused, and therefore only those initiated into the mysteries of the brotherhood were entrusted with these sacred truths.

The symbolic language of alchemy found in Rosicrucian writings is rich with references to divine transformation. The imagery of the rose and the cross, central to Rosicrucian symbolism, reflects this alchemical process. The rose, a symbol of beauty, purity, and spiritual awakening, represents the soul's unfolding during the process of enlightenment, while the cross symbolizes the material world, suffering, and death. Together, the rose and the cross encapsulate the essence of the alchemical journey—the soul's transcendence of the material world through divine suffering, resulting in spiritual rebirth. This theme of death and rebirth, present in both alchemy and Rosicrucian teachings, echoes the universal cycle of transformation that all seekers must undergo.

The practice of spiritual alchemy in the Rosicrucian tradition also emphasizes the importance of balance between the inner and outer worlds. The Rosicrucians understood that the external world of matter is a reflection of the internal world of the soul, and that transformation in one leads to transformation in the other. This belief is closely tied to the Hermetic principle of "as above, so below," which asserts that the macrocosm of the universe and the microcosm of the individual are interconnected. For the Rosicrucian adept, the alchemical process is a holistic one, involving not just inner contemplation and spiritual practice but also engagement with the natural world and the study of its mysteries.

The pursuit of alchemical transformation in Rosicrucianism is ultimately a quest for divine union. It is through this process of inner purification, dissolution, and reintegration that the seeker comes to embody the divine within themselves. Alchemy, for the Rosicrucians, is the means by which the soul is restored to its original, pure state, before its descent into the material world. The teachings of the Rosy Cross, with their emphasis on alchemical symbolism and spiritual transformation, offer a path to achieving this divine union—a journey that requires not only knowledge and wisdom but also perseverance, humility, and faith in the hidden processes of the universe.

Chapter 7: The Rosicrucian Manifestos: Defining the Brotherhood's Purpose

The Rosicrucian manifestos, published in the early 17th century, are foundational texts that define the purpose, philosophy, and mission of the secretive brotherhood known as the Rosicrucians. These three key documents—the *Fama Fraternitatis* (1614), the *Confessio Fraternitatis* (1615), and *The Chymical Wedding of Christian Rosenkreuz* (1617)—outlined the ideals of the Rosicrucian Order and provided a vision for the transformation of science, religion, and society. Each manifesto introduced the figure of Christian Rosenkreuz, the legendary founder of the order, and portrayed the brotherhood as a group of enlightened individuals dedicated to the betterment of humanity through spiritual, intellectual, and moral reform.

The *Fama Fraternitatis*, the first of the manifestos, serves as an introduction to the existence and history of the Rosicrucian Brotherhood. It recounts the life of Christian Rosenkreuz, a German nobleman who, after traveling through the Middle East and learning the secret wisdom of the East, returned to Europe with the desire to share his knowledge. Rosenkreuz, disillusioned by the ignorance and corruption he encountered upon his return, established a small, secret brotherhood devoted to the pursuit of divine knowledge, healing, and the reformation of society. The *Fama* declares that the time has come for the brotherhood to reveal itself to the world, calling on those with the intellectual and spiritual capacity to join their cause.

The purpose of the *Fama Fraternitatis* goes beyond merely introducing the brotherhood; it critiques the existing institutions of Europe, particularly the Church and universities, for their failure to promote true knowledge and wisdom. The Rosicrucians saw these institutions as being bogged down by dogma, superstition, and a refusal to embrace new ideas. The manifesto calls for a reform of knowledge and spirituality, one that integrates science, religion, and philosophy into a unified pursuit of truth. In this vision, the Rosicrucians present themselves as the vanguard of this new era of enlightenment, possessing secret knowledge that could heal the divisions in society and restore harmony between humanity and the divine.

The second manifesto, the *Confessio Fraternitatis*, elaborates on the ideals set forth in the *Fama* and reinforces the brotherhood's commitment to the reformation of knowledge and society. While the *Fama* introduces the brotherhood and its goals, the *Confessio* serves as a declaration of the Rosicrucians' spiritual philosophy and their rejection of the materialism and corruption they believed dominated European institutions. The *Confessio* emphasizes the Rosicrucians' belief in the importance of divine revelation and the study of nature as the means to access higher truths. It also reaffirms the brotherhood's commitment to secrecy, stating that the true teachings of the order will only be revealed to those who are spiritually ready to receive them.

The *Confessio* also touches on the Rosicrucian interpretation of alchemy, not as a quest for material wealth but as a metaphor for spiritual transformation. For the Rosicrucians, the alchemical process of turning base metals into gold symbolized the purification of the soul and the attainment of divine wisdom. This spiritual alchemy, central to Rosicrucian teachings, is presented as a path to enlightenment, where the seeker undergoes a series of trials and transformations to achieve union with the divine. The manifesto emphasizes that this knowledge is not for everyone, only for those who have undergone the necessary spiritual preparation and inner purification.

The Chymical Wedding of Christian Rosenkreuz, the third manifesto, takes a different approach from the *Fama* and *Confessio*. Rather than a straightforward declaration of the brotherhood's purpose, *The Chymical Wedding* is an allegorical tale that represents the alchemical process of spiritual transformation. The story follows Christian Rosenkreuz as he is invited to attend a mysterious wedding at a distant castle, a journey filled with symbolic trials and challenges. The wedding itself represents the union of opposites, a core theme in alchemy, where masculine and feminine, spiritual and material, are reconciled. The allegory reflects the Rosicrucian belief in the possibility of personal and cosmic harmony through the integration of dualities.

The *Chymical Wedding* is filled with alchemical symbolism, much of which is open to interpretation. However, its underlying message is consistent with the previous two manifestos: the journey toward spiritual enlightenment is a complex and transformative process, requiring both personal effort and divine guidance. The challenges faced by Christian Rosenkreuz on his journey to the wedding reflect the internal struggles of the seeker, who must overcome ignorance, pride, and material attachment in order to achieve true wisdom. The wedding itself, a symbol of alchemical conjunction, represents the culmination of the spiritual journey, where the seeker attains a state of divine union and enlightenment.

Throughout the manifestos, the Rosicrucian Brotherhood is portrayed as a group of enlightened individuals working in secret to bring about a new era of knowledge and spiritual awakening. The manifestos emphasize that the Rosicrucians do not seek personal fame or material wealth; their goal is the betterment of humanity through the dissemination of hidden wisdom and the reformation of society. The brotherhood operates in secrecy, not out of elitism, but because they believe that true wisdom is not for the masses. Only those who have undergone the necessary spiritual preparation are capable of understanding and applying the teachings of the Rosicrucians.

The Rosicrucian manifestos had a profound impact on the intellectual and spiritual climate of Europe. They ignited debates about the existence of the brotherhood, the nature of their teachings, and the possibility of a hidden group of enlightened individuals working behind the scenes to reform society. Many saw the manifestos as a call to join a real organization, while others interpreted them as a metaphor for a broader spiritual movement. Regardless of their true origins, the Rosicrucian manifestos laid the foundation for modern esoteric thought, influencing not only later occult traditions such as Freemasonry and the Hermetic Order of the Golden Dawn, but also the development of modern science and philosophy.

Chapter 8: European Reformation and the Rosicrucian Influence

The European Reformation was a period of profound upheaval in religious, intellectual, and social life, characterized by the fracturing of the Catholic Church and the emergence of Protestantism. During this time, various reform movements sought to challenge the established authority of the Church, advocating for a return to spiritual purity and a more personal relationship with the divine. It was in this context of religious transformation and intellectual ferment that the Rosicrucian manifestos appeared, offering a unique blend of mystical thought, alchemical teachings, and calls for reform. The Rosicrucians, though shrouded in secrecy, exerted a significant influence on the intellectual and spiritual currents of the time, helping to shape the broader cultural shift toward new modes of thinking in both religion and science.

The Reformation, which began in the early 16th century with figures like Martin Luther and John Calvin, aimed to challenge the corruption and dogma of the Catholic Church. Reformers sought to strip away the excesses of the Church, advocating for a more direct relationship between the individual and God, based on personal faith and the authority of the Bible. This push for spiritual reform resonated with the Rosicrucian ideal of an enlightened brotherhood devoted to the pursuit of hidden knowledge and the reformation of society. While the Rosicrucians were not explicitly tied to the Protestant Reformation, their teachings echoed many of the same concerns about the corruption of established institutions and the need for spiritual renewal.

The Rosicrucian manifestos, published in the early 17th century, proposed a vision of a new world, where science, religion, and philosophy were united in the pursuit of truth and enlightenment. This vision was deeply influenced by the intellectual climate of the Reformation, which emphasized personal spiritual development and the rejection of religious authority that was seen as corrupt or out of touch with the divine. The Rosicrucians sought to establish a spiritual reformation that went beyond the Protestant critique of the Catholic Church. They aimed for a transformation of all aspects of life, advocating for a new approach to science, philosophy, and the study of nature that would reveal the hidden truths of the universe.

One of the key ways in which the Rosicrucian movement aligned with the Reformation was in its emphasis on personal revelation and the direct experience of the divine. Just as the Protestant reformers called for individuals to read and interpret the Bible for themselves, bypassing the mediation of the clergy, the Rosicrucians promoted the idea that divine wisdom could be accessed through personal spiritual practice and study. They believed that true knowledge was not confined to religious texts or the teachings of the Church but could be found in the natural world and through inner spiritual development. This idea reflected the broader Reformation spirit of challenging established authority and seeking a more direct connection to spiritual truth.

The Rosicrucian emphasis on alchemy and natural philosophy also mirrored the Reformation's call for a return to the purity of early Christianity. Just as Protestant reformers sought to strip away the layers of tradition that had accumulated over centuries in the Church, the Rosicrucians advocated for a return to a more ancient and pure understanding of the natural world. They believed that the secrets of the universe were encoded in nature, waiting to be discovered through a combination of scientific inquiry and mystical insight. This blending of science and mysticism was a hallmark of the Rosicrucian worldview, which sought to unite the physical and spiritual in a harmonious pursuit of enlightenment.

The intellectual climate of the European Reformation also provided fertile ground for the Rosicrucian ideals of secrecy and initiation. The fracturing of religious authority during the Reformation led to the rise of various secret societies and underground movements, as individuals sought alternative ways to explore their spiritual and intellectual ideas outside the constraints of mainstream institutions. The Rosicrucians, with their emphasis on a hidden brotherhood working in secret to reform the world, fit neatly into this landscape of clandestine networks and esoteric knowledge. Their insistence that only the spiritually prepared could join their ranks echoed the Reformation's emphasis on personal faith and inner conviction.

The influence of the Rosicrucian movement on the broader intellectual life of Europe during and after the Reformation was significant. The publication of the Rosicrucian manifestos ignited a wave of interest in esoteric traditions, alchemy, and the search for hidden knowledge. Many scholars and thinkers of the time, particularly those involved in early scientific endeavors, were drawn to the Rosicrucian ideals of a unified science that combined natural philosophy, spirituality, and mysticism. Figures like Robert Fludd, a prominent English physician and mystical thinker, were heavily influenced by Rosicrucian ideas, which shaped their contributions to the developing fields of science and medicine. Fludd's work on the interconnectedness of the cosmos and the human body reflected the Rosicrucian belief in the microcosm-macrocosm relationship, where the individual was seen as a reflection of the larger universe.

The Rosicrucian influence extended into the realms of art, literature, and politics as well. Many writers and artists of the time were inspired by the symbolism and ideals of the Rosicrucians, incorporating elements of their mystical philosophy into their works. The Rosicrucians' call for a new, enlightened world order also resonated with political thinkers, particularly during the turbulent times of the Thirty Years' War, when Europe was ravaged by religious conflict. The idea of a secret brotherhood working for the betterment of humanity through hidden wisdom offered a compelling alternative to the chaos and division that characterized much of the period.

The Rosicrucians' influence on the European Reformation and the intellectual movements that followed cannot be understated. While they remained elusive and secretive, their ideals of personal spiritual enlightenment, the reformation of society, and the pursuit of hidden knowledge resonated deeply with the intellectual and spiritual currents of the time. As Europe continued to grapple with the religious and political upheavals of the Reformation, the Rosicrucian vision of a new world order, based on divine wisdom and the union of science and spirituality, remained a powerful force in shaping the cultural and intellectual landscape of the early modern period.

Chapter 9: Rosicrucianism and Freemasonry: Interwoven Mysteries

Rosicrucianism and Freemasonry, two of the most influential and enigmatic esoteric traditions in Western history, share numerous connections in their symbolism, philosophy, and organizational structures. Both movements arose from similar cultural and intellectual contexts and have influenced each other in significant ways. While Rosicrucianism emerged in the early 17th century with the publication of its manifestos, Freemasonry has roots that stretch back even further, drawing from medieval stonemason guilds. Despite their different origins, the two traditions have become interwoven over time, particularly through their shared emphasis on initiation, secrecy, and the pursuit of spiritual enlightenment. This connection has led many to speculate that the Rosicrucian movement played a key role in shaping the development of modern Freemasonry, infusing it with mystical elements and a deeper spiritual philosophy.

One of the most striking parallels between Rosicrucianism and Freemasonry is their use of allegory and symbolism to convey esoteric truths. Both traditions employ rich symbolic language, often drawing on similar motifs such as the use of geometric figures, sacred architecture, and references to ancient wisdom. In Rosicrucianism, the rose and the cross are central symbols, representing the union of material and spiritual, death and resurrection, and the unfolding of divine wisdom. Freemasonry, on the other hand, uses symbols like the compass, square, and the unfinished temple to represent the building of the inner spiritual self. Both movements place a strong emphasis on the idea of personal transformation and the refinement of the soul, often described in alchemical or architectural terms.

Freemasonry's symbolic references to the construction of Solomon's Temple echo the Rosicrucian vision of spiritual and intellectual building. The idea of constructing a sacred temple, whether it is physical or metaphorical, is present in both traditions. For Rosicrucians, the construction of a temple symbolizes the inner work of spiritual development, where the individual builds themselves into a reflection of divine order and harmony. In Freemasonry, this theme manifests in the allegory of the master mason, who is engaged in the work of building not just a physical structure but a moral and spiritual edifice within. The unfinished nature of the temple represents the ongoing process of personal growth and enlightenment, a theme that resonates with the Rosicrucian commitment to continuous spiritual transformation.

The ritualistic structure of both Rosicrucianism and Freemasonry is another important area of connection. Both traditions operate through a system of initiation, where individuals must undergo a series of symbolic rites to gain access to the deeper mysteries of the organization. In Rosicrucianism, initiation often involves the study of alchemical and mystical texts, along with personal spiritual practices aimed at refining the soul. Freemasonry similarly employs a graded system of initiation, where members progress through different degrees, each of which reveals new symbolic knowledge and deeper understanding of the Masonic philosophy. This focus on initiation and gradual revelation reflects the belief, shared by both traditions, that spiritual enlightenment is a process that requires dedication, discipline, and the guidance of those who have already advanced on the path.

The Rosicrucian manifestos, particularly the *Fama Fraternitatis* and *Confessio Fraternitatis*, outline a vision of a secret brotherhood working behind the scenes to reform society through the dissemination of hidden wisdom. This vision mirrors the early development of Freemasonry, where the idea of a secret fraternity dedicated to moral and intellectual improvement played a central role. While Freemasonry did not initially present itself as an esoteric movement in the same way Rosicrucianism did, the incorporation of mystical and alchemical ideas into Masonic rituals and teachings occurred gradually, influenced in part by the rise of Rosicrucianism and other occult movements in the early modern period. By the 18th century, Freemasonry had adopted many of the same themes that were central to Rosicrucian thought, including the belief in the importance of hidden knowledge and the role of the individual in the spiritual and moral transformation of society.

One of the clearest examples of the intersection between Rosicrucianism and Freemasonry is the emergence of the Scottish Rite, one of the most well-known and influential branches of Freemasonry. The Scottish Rite, which developed in the 18th century, includes several degrees that incorporate Rosicrucian themes and symbolism. The 18th degree of the Scottish Rite, known as the Knight of the Rose Croix, is explicitly connected to Rosicrucianism, drawing on its alchemical and mystical imagery. In this degree, the initiate is introduced to the concept of the rose and the cross as symbols of spiritual enlightenment and the process of resurrection or rebirth. The influence of Rosicrucian ideas in the Scottish Rite demonstrates how deeply the two traditions have become intertwined, with Freemasonry adopting and adapting Rosicrucian symbolism to fit its own system of moral and philosophical teachings.

The shared emphasis on moral and intellectual improvement also highlights the broader cultural and philosophical context in which both Rosicrucianism and Freemasonry developed. During the Renaissance and early modern period, Europe was undergoing a transformation in terms of how knowledge was understood and disseminated. The rise of humanism, the rediscovery of classical texts, and the development of natural philosophy all contributed to a new intellectual climate that valued personal inquiry, the study of nature, and the pursuit of hidden truths. Rosicrucianism and Freemasonry both emerged as responses to this cultural shift, offering alternative paths to knowledge that combined ancient wisdom with new scientific and philosophical ideas. In this sense, both movements can be seen as part of a broader intellectual tradition that sought to reconcile the spiritual and the material, the mystical and the rational, in the quest for human enlightenment.

The relationship between Rosicrucianism and Freemasonry, while complex, reflects a shared commitment to the pursuit of wisdom, the transformation of the self, and the betterment of society. Though each tradition developed independently, they have influenced and enriched each other over the centuries, contributing to the development of Western esoteric thought and shaping the spiritual landscape of the modern world. Both movements continue to attract individuals who seek not only personal growth but also a deeper understanding of the mysteries of the universe and humanity's place within it.

Chapter 10: From Myth to Legacy: The Enduring Appeal of the Rosicrucian Order

The Rosicrucian Order has captured the imagination of mystics, philosophers, and seekers of hidden wisdom for centuries. Its origins, shrouded in mystery and myth, have lent an aura of intrigue to its history, and its teachings, steeped in esoteric knowledge, have had a lasting influence on both the intellectual and spiritual traditions of the Western world. The Rosicrucians, first introduced to the world through a series of manifestos in the early 17th century, have been portrayed as a secret brotherhood dedicated to the pursuit of divine wisdom, the reformation of society, and the unlocking of the hidden mysteries of nature. Over time, the myth surrounding the Rosicrucians has grown, and their legacy has endured, as their ideals continue to resonate with those drawn to spiritual and intellectual exploration.

One of the most compelling aspects of the Rosicrucian myth is the figure of Christian Rosenkreuz, the legendary founder of the order. Rosenkreuz is described in the *Fama Fraternitatis* as a German nobleman who, after traveling through the Middle East and learning the wisdom of the ancients, returned to Europe to share his knowledge. He founded a secret society, the Rosicrucian Brotherhood, which would work in anonymity to reform science, religion, and society. The legend of Rosenkreuz is rich with allegory, and many scholars believe that his story is not meant to be taken literally but symbolically, representing the journey of spiritual awakening and enlightenment. The name "Rosenkreuz" itself, a combination of the rose and the cross, is laden with symbolic meaning, reflecting themes of death, rebirth, and the blossoming of divine wisdom.

The Rosicrucian manifestos, particularly the *Fama Fraternitatis*, *Confessio Fraternitatis*, and *The Chymical Wedding of Christian Rosenkreuz*, laid the foundation for the myth of the Rosicrucian Order. These texts introduced the world to the idea of a hidden brotherhood working behind the scenes to bring about a new era of knowledge and enlightenment. The manifestos were written in a time of great intellectual and religious upheaval in Europe, during the Renaissance and the Protestant Reformation, when new ideas were challenging the established order. The Rosicrucians, through their manifestos, called for a reformation not only of religion but of science and philosophy, proposing a vision of a world where divine wisdom, nature, and human reason were harmoniously united.

The allure of the Rosicrucian Order lies in its blending of mysticism, science, and spiritual transformation. At a time when science was emerging as a distinct field of inquiry, separate from religion, the Rosicrucians offered an alternative vision where the study of the natural world was deeply intertwined with the pursuit of spiritual knowledge. Alchemy, a central theme in Rosicrucian thought, was not just the transmutation of metals but a metaphor for the transformation of the soul. The process of turning base metals into gold symbolized the purification and enlightenment of the individual, a theme that resonated with the spiritual seekers of the time. This emphasis on spiritual alchemy continues to be one of the most enduring appeals of Rosicrucianism.

The Rosicrucians' focus on secrecy and initiation also contributed to their mystique. The idea that the true teachings of the order were hidden and could only be accessed by those who were spiritually prepared has drawn countless individuals to seek initiation into their mysteries. This exclusivity, combined with the promise of hidden wisdom, has been a powerful draw for those who are dissatisfied with conventional religious or philosophical teachings and seek deeper spiritual truths. The Rosicrucian manifestos suggest that their knowledge is not for the masses but for the few who are ready to receive it, a notion that has contributed to the sense of mystery and allure that surrounds the order.

Throughout history, the Rosicrucian Order has inspired a wide range of interpretations and adaptations. During the Enlightenment, the ideals of the Rosicrucians, particularly their focus on reason, science, and spiritual enlightenment, influenced a number of intellectual and esoteric movements. Freemasonry, for example, incorporated many Rosicrucian themes, including the use of allegory, symbols, and the idea of moral and spiritual transformation through initiation. The Hermetic Order of the Golden Dawn, a 19th-century esoteric society, also drew heavily on Rosicrucian teachings, particularly in its emphasis on alchemy, ritual magic, and the pursuit of hidden knowledge.

The Rosicrucian legacy has also had a lasting impact on modern occultism and New Age spirituality. The teachings of the Rosicrucians, with their emphasis on personal transformation, the study of nature, and the interconnectedness of all things, resonate with many contemporary spiritual movements. The idea that spiritual enlightenment is a process of inner transformation, where the individual must undergo trials and purifications in order to attain higher wisdom, is a central tenet of both traditional Rosicrucian thought and modern esoteric practices. This focus on self-directed spiritual growth continues to attract individuals who are searching for a path to personal and cosmic harmony.

Even in the modern era, where science and rationalism often dominate, the myth of the Rosicrucians endures, drawing those who are fascinated by the possibility of hidden truths and esoteric wisdom. Organizations that claim descent from the original Rosicrucian Brotherhood continue to exist, offering teachings and practices that align with the ideals laid out in the original manifestos. Whether these groups are directly connected to the historical Rosicrucians or not, they carry forward the legacy of the Rosy Cross, perpetuating its ideals of spiritual transformation, intellectual inquiry, and the pursuit of divine wisdom.

The enduring appeal of the Rosicrucian Order, from its mysterious beginnings to its continued influence on modern spiritual and esoteric thought, reflects a deep human desire for connection with something greater than the material world. The promise of hidden knowledge, the allure of initiation into a secret brotherhood, and the quest for personal and spiritual transformation continue to captivate those who seek to understand the mysteries of the universe and their place within it. The Rosicrucian myth, with its potent blend of mysticism, philosophy, and science, remains a powerful symbol of the ongoing search for enlightenment and wisdom.

BOOK 2
ALCHEMY AND THE ROSICRUCIAN TRADITION:
UNLOCKING THE HIDDEN SYMBOLS
SAMUEL SHEPHERD

Chapter 1: The Alchemical Origins: Foundations of the Rosicrucian Quest

The origins of the Rosicrucian quest are deeply rooted in the tradition of alchemy, a system of thought that combined elements of mysticism, philosophy, and proto-science in its exploration of the natural world and the transformation of both matter and spirit. Alchemy, often seen as the precursor to modern chemistry, was far more than the pursuit of turning base metals into gold. It was, at its core, a spiritual practice that sought to reveal the hidden connections between the material and divine realms. This esoteric tradition became the foundation upon which the Rosicrucians built their quest for enlightenment, inner transformation, and universal harmony.

Alchemy provided the symbolic and conceptual framework that shaped Rosicrucian thought. Central to the practice of alchemy is the concept of transmutation, a process by which matter is purified and perfected. In alchemical terms, this could refer to the literal transformation of lead into gold, but on a deeper level, it symbolized the transformation of the human soul from a base, earthly state to one of spiritual enlightenment. This concept resonated strongly with the Rosicrucians, who saw their mission as not only the pursuit of scientific knowledge but also the elevation of the soul through spiritual purification. The Great Work, or *Magnum Opus*, of alchemy became synonymous with the Rosicrucian path to enlightenment, where the adept would undergo a series of trials and transformations, mirroring the stages of alchemical transmutation, in order to achieve spiritual perfection.

One of the key alchemical processes that influenced Rosicrucian thought is the idea of the alchemical wedding or the union of opposites. In alchemy, this refers to the conjunction of masculine and feminine principles, represented by the symbols of the sun and moon, which together create a harmonious and unified whole. The Rosicrucians adopted this concept, interpreting it as the reconciliation of material and spiritual forces. For the Rosicrucians, the alchemical wedding symbolized the integration of the physical body with the spiritual soul, a union that leads to enlightenment. This idea is central to Rosicrucian philosophy, where the quest for knowledge and truth involves balancing the dualities of existence—light and dark, spirit and matter, intellect and intuition—in order to achieve a higher state of being.

The Rosicrucian quest is also deeply informed by the alchemical belief in the microcosm and macrocosm. Alchemists believed that the individual (microcosm) reflected the structure and processes of the universe (macrocosm), and that by studying the natural world, one could gain insight into the divine order of creation. This principle became a cornerstone of Rosicrucian philosophy, where the study of nature and the cosmos was seen as a pathway to divine knowledge. The

Rosicrucians believed that the material world was imbued with hidden truths, and that by unlocking these secrets, they could reveal the divine laws governing both the universe and the human soul. The idea that the macrocosm and microcosm were interconnected also reinforced the Rosicrucian commitment to the idea of personal transformation as a reflection of universal harmony. By purifying and transforming themselves, the Rosicrucians believed they could align with the greater cosmic order and play a role in the reformation of the world.

Alchemy's emphasis on symbolism and allegory also shaped the Rosicrucian approach to knowledge and initiation. The alchemical texts were often written in obscure language, filled with symbolic images and metaphors, intended to be deciphered only by those who had undergone the necessary spiritual preparation. This method of encoding knowledge in symbols and allegory was adopted by the Rosicrucians, who believed that true wisdom could not be easily communicated or understood by the uninitiated. Their manifestos, particularly *The Chymical Wedding of Christian Rosenkreuz*, are rich with alchemical symbolism, designed to convey spiritual truths in a hidden form. For the Rosicrucians, the process of initiation into their mysteries was akin to the alchemical process itself: just as base metals must be purified and transmuted, so too must the initiate undergo a series of inner transformations before they could attain higher knowledge.

The influence of alchemy on the Rosicrucians is also evident in their focus on healing, both physical and spiritual. Alchemy was often referred to as the "art of healing," and many alchemists were also physicians who sought to cure diseases through the use of herbal remedies and the understanding of the body's connection to the cosmos. The Rosicrucians, drawing on this alchemical tradition, saw healing as a key component of their quest. They believed that the knowledge of alchemical principles could be applied to the healing of the human body, just as it could be applied to the healing of the soul. This holistic approach to healing, which combined physical remedies with spiritual practices, was central to the Rosicrucian mission of bringing about a reformation of both the individual and society.

The Rosicrucian emphasis on secrecy and initiation also has its roots in alchemical tradition. Just as alchemical knowledge was considered too powerful and dangerous to be widely disseminated, the Rosicrucians believed that their teachings should only be accessible to those who were spiritually prepared to receive them. This belief in the selective revelation of knowledge is reflected in the Rosicrucian practice of initiation, where individuals must undergo a series of rites and tests before they are admitted to the inner circle of the brotherhood. The secrecy surrounding the Rosicrucian order and its teachings helped to preserve its esoteric nature, ensuring that its wisdom would remain hidden from those who were not ready to understand it.

The foundations of the Rosicrucian quest, deeply rooted in alchemical tradition, represent a synthesis of science, mysticism, and spiritual practice. The Rosicrucians took the principles of alchemy—transmutation, the union of opposites, the microcosm and macrocosm, healing, and the use of symbolic language—and adapted them into a system of thought that sought to bridge the gap between the material and the spiritual, the physical and the divine. This alchemical foundation continues to influence the enduring legacy of the Rosicrucians, whose quest for enlightenment and universal harmony remains a powerful symbol of the ongoing human desire for transformation and higher knowledge.

Chapter 2: The Philosopher's Stone: Symbol of Spiritual Perfection

The Philosopher's Stone, one of the most enduring and enigmatic symbols in the alchemical tradition, has long represented the ultimate goal of alchemy: the ability to transform base metals into gold and, more significantly, the attainment of spiritual perfection. While the material transformation of lead into gold was often taken literally by those unfamiliar with the deeper teachings of alchemy, the true essence of the Philosopher's Stone lies in its symbolic meaning. It represents the process of inner purification and spiritual enlightenment, the journey of the soul toward divine knowledge and transcendence. For alchemists and, later, for esoteric traditions like Rosicrucianism, the Philosopher's Stone became a metaphor for the ultimate state of spiritual perfection, where the individual achieves harmony with the divine and transcends the limitations of the material world.

The symbolism of the Philosopher's Stone is rooted in the alchemical belief that all matter contains within it the potential for transformation. Just as base metals can be transmuted into gold through a series of alchemical processes, so too can the human soul undergo a similar transformation, evolving from a state of impurity and ignorance to one of purity and enlightenment. The Philosopher's Stone, in this context, represents the final stage of the *Magnum Opus*, or Great Work, where the alchemist—whether a literal or figurative seeker—has completed the process of purification and achieved a state of spiritual perfection. This idea of spiritual transmutation became central to alchemical philosophy, and the quest for the Philosopher's Stone became synonymous with the quest for self-realization and enlightenment.

In alchemical texts, the Philosopher's Stone is often described as possessing miraculous properties, not only capable of transforming metals into gold but also of bestowing immortality and divine wisdom. These descriptions are filled with metaphorical significance. The ability to turn lead into gold symbolizes the refinement of the soul, where the alchemist, through discipline, meditation, and inner work, overcomes the base instincts and desires that bind them to the material world. The immortality conferred by the Philosopher's Stone is not simply a physical extension of life, but a representation of the soul's eternal nature, which is revealed once the individual has transcended the limitations of the physical body and attained unity with the divine. The wisdom gained through the possession of the Philosopher's Stone is the ultimate understanding of the laws that govern both the material and spiritual realms.

The process of creating the Philosopher's Stone in alchemical texts is described in stages, each representing a phase of spiritual development. These stages—commonly known as *nigredo* (blackening), *albedo* (whitening), *citrinitas* (yellowing), and *rubedo* (reddening)—mirror the psychological and spiritual purification the alchemist must undergo. The *nigredo* stage represents the initial destruction of the ego and the confrontation with one's own inner darkness. This is a period of dissolution, where the individual's attachment to the material world and their lower instincts are burned away, leaving only the essence of the true self. This phase is often associated with the idea of spiritual death, where the individual must let go of their former identity to make way for a higher state of being.

The next stage, *albedo*, symbolizes the purification of the soul. In this phase, the alchemist begins to experience inner clarity and enlightenment, as the impurities of the ego have been removed, and the individual is now more in tune with the divine. This is often described as a state of spiritual rebirth, where the soul is cleansed and made ready to receive higher truths. The *albedo* phase represents the illumination of the inner self, a moment of spiritual awakening where the individual begins to perceive the unity between themselves and the cosmos.

Citrinitas, the yellowing stage, marks the transition from illumination to the integration of divine wisdom. In this phase, the alchemist begins to internalize the spiritual insights they have gained, and these insights start to manifest in their life and actions. The symbolism of yellow, often associated with the sun, reflects the dawning of a new consciousness, where the individual's understanding of the divine order becomes more complete. This phase is crucial for the alchemist, as it represents the beginning of the process of turning knowledge into wisdom, and bringing that wisdom into the material world.

The final stage, *rubedo*, or reddening, represents the culmination of the alchemical process—the creation of the Philosopher's Stone itself. In this phase, the alchemist achieves spiritual perfection, where the soul is fully aligned with the divine, and the individual has transcended the dualities of the material and spiritual realms. The red color of this stage symbolizes the life force and the union of opposites, the harmonious integration of spirit and matter. The alchemist, having completed the Great Work, is now in possession of the Philosopher's Stone, not as a physical object, but as a symbol of their own enlightened state.

The Philosopher's Stone, as a symbol, extends beyond the realm of alchemy and has been embraced by various esoteric traditions, including Rosicrucianism. For the Rosicrucians, the Stone represented the pinnacle of spiritual attainment, the embodiment of the ideals of purification, enlightenment, and union with the divine. The Rosicrucian quest for the Philosopher's Stone was not a search for material wealth, but a metaphor for the journey of the soul toward higher consciousness and the discovery of the divine wisdom that lies hidden within the individual. In Rosicrucian philosophy, the process of seeking the Philosopher's Stone is closely linked to the alchemical transformation of the self, where the individual must undergo a series of spiritual trials to purify their soul and prepare for the reception of divine knowledge.

The enduring power of the Philosopher's Stone as a symbol of spiritual perfection lies in its ability to encapsulate the entire alchemical process of transformation. It represents not just the final goal of the alchemist's quest, but also the journey itself, with all its stages of purification, enlightenment, and integration. The Philosopher's Stone serves as a reminder that the path to spiritual perfection is a process of inner alchemy, where the individual must confront their own darkness, purify their soul, and ultimately transcend the limitations of the material world to achieve unity with the divine. Through this lens, the Philosopher's Stone continues to inspire seekers on their spiritual journeys, offering a powerful symbol of the potential for transformation and the realization of one's true divine nature.

Chapter 3: The Emerald Tablet: Unveiling the Rosicrucian Code

The *Emerald Tablet* has long held a revered place within the traditions of alchemy and esoteric thought, particularly among the Rosicrucians, who saw in its cryptic verses a reflection of their own mystical philosophy. Attributed to Hermes Trismegistus, a figure associated with the fusion of Greek and Egyptian wisdom, the *Emerald Tablet* encapsulates the core principles of alchemy in just a few brief lines. Its most famous maxim, "As above, so below," resonates deeply with Rosicrucian teachings, expressing the fundamental idea that the macrocosm of the universe is reflected in the microcosm of the human soul. For the Rosicrucians, the *Emerald Tablet* was not merely a document about physical alchemy but a profound spiritual guide, providing insight into the nature of the cosmos and the process of personal transformation.

The origins of the *Emerald Tablet* are shrouded in mystery, much like the origins of the Rosicrucian Order itself. While the Tablet's content is often traced back to the Hellenistic period, its themes draw heavily on older Hermetic and Egyptian traditions, blending elements of mysticism, alchemical practice, and spiritual philosophy. The Rosicrucians, who emerged during the early 17th century with the publication of their manifestos, found in the *Emerald Tablet* a perfect expression of their own esoteric beliefs. Both the Rosicrucian manifestos and the *Emerald Tablet* shared a common goal: the unification of spiritual and material realms, the elevation of human consciousness, and the search for hidden truths within the fabric of nature.

The phrase "As above, so below" serves as the cornerstone of the *Emerald Tablet* and encapsulates one of the most essential tenets of both alchemy and Rosicrucian thought. In Rosicrucianism, this principle is interpreted as the idea that everything in the material world is a reflection of the divine order that exists on a higher plane. Just as the stars and planets influence the physical world, the actions of individuals on Earth mirror the larger cosmic forces at play. This belief in the interconnectedness of all things underpins the Rosicrucian approach to both science and spirituality. The Rosicrucians saw the study of nature and the cosmos not as separate from spiritual practice but as integral to the process of enlightenment. By understanding the laws that govern the material world, the Rosicrucian adept could also gain insight into the divine mysteries that lay beyond.

The *Emerald Tablet* also speaks of the process of transmutation, a theme that is central to Rosicrucian philosophy. In alchemical terms, transmutation refers to the transformation of base metals into gold, but for the Rosicrucians, this process was understood primarily as a metaphor for the purification of the soul. The Tablet's description of a "One Thing" that permeates all existence reflects the Rosicrucian belief in a divine essence that flows through every aspect of creation. This essence, sometimes referred to as the "Universal Spirit" or "Quintessence," was thought to be the substance from which both the material and spiritual worlds were formed. The Rosicrucians believed that by tapping into this essence, they could initiate the process of transmutation within themselves, purifying their souls and aligning their consciousness with the divine order.

The reference to the "One Thing" in the *Emerald Tablet* also aligns with the Rosicrucian view of the unity of all knowledge. The Rosicrucians rejected the rigid divisions between science, religion, and philosophy that characterized much of the intellectual landscape of their time. For them, all fields of study were interconnected, and true wisdom could only be attained by understanding the relationships between them. The Rosicrucian belief in the unity of knowledge was inspired in part by the Hermetic tradition, which taught that the mysteries of the cosmos could be unlocked through a synthesis of intellectual, spiritual, and experiential knowledge. The *Emerald Tablet*, with its emphasis on the unity of all things, reinforced this idea and provided a framework for the Rosicrucian quest to harmonize scientific inquiry with spiritual insight.

Another key concept in the *Emerald Tablet* that resonated with Rosicrucian teachings is the idea of the "Great Work." In alchemical practice, the Great Work refers to the process of creating the Philosopher's

Stone, the substance believed to grant immortality and ultimate wisdom. For the Rosicrucians, the Great Work symbolized the inner alchemical process of self-transformation. This involved not only the purification of the soul but also the development of intellectual and moral virtues. The Rosicrucians believed that through meditation, study, and the practice of alchemical principles, the individual could undergo a series of spiritual transformations that would eventually lead to enlightenment. The *Emerald Tablet* describes this process in veiled language, offering clues to the adept about the stages of transformation necessary to achieve spiritual perfection.

The relationship between the Sun and the Moon, as described in the *Emerald Tablet*, also plays a significant role in Rosicrucian symbolism. In alchemical and Rosicrucian thought, the Sun represents the active, masculine principle, while the Moon represents the passive, feminine principle. The interplay between these two forces is essential for the process of creation and transmutation. The Rosicrucians, who placed great importance on the reconciliation of opposites, saw the union of the Sun and Moon as symbolic of the integration of the spiritual and material realms, as well as the balance between intellect and intuition. The idea of the alchemical wedding, in which these two forces are brought together in harmony, was central to both the *Emerald Tablet* and Rosicrucian philosophy.

The *Emerald Tablet* also alludes to the role of the alchemist or adept as a mediator between the material and spiritual worlds. This idea is echoed in Rosicrucian thought, where the initiate is seen as a bridge between the divine and the earthly, capable of tapping into higher realms of consciousness while remaining grounded in the material world. The Rosicrucians believed that the adept, through their understanding of alchemical principles, could help to bring about a transformation not only within themselves but also within society as a whole. This mission of spiritual and societal reformation, as outlined in the Rosicrucian manifestos, was seen as the ultimate goal of the Rosicrucian quest.

The teachings of the *Emerald Tablet* and their profound influence on Rosicrucianism illustrate the deep connection between alchemical philosophy and the Rosicrucian code. Both traditions emphasized the transformative power of knowledge, the unity of all things, and the potential for human beings to achieve spiritual perfection through the process of inner and outer alchemy. Through the cryptic verses of the *Emerald Tablet*, the Rosicrucians found a guide to unlocking the mysteries of the universe and aligning their quest for enlightenment with the divine order of creation. The Tablet's enduring wisdom continues to inspire those drawn to the mysteries of alchemy and the pursuit of spiritual transformation.

Chapter 4: Prima Materia: The Sacred Essence in Alchemy

In the alchemical tradition, *prima materia* represents the fundamental, undifferentiated substance from which all things originate. It is often described as the raw material of creation, the source from which the alchemist begins the process of transformation. This concept lies at the heart of alchemical practice, symbolizing both the physical and spiritual potential that exists in a raw, unformed state. For alchemists, the *prima materia* is not only the starting point for the transmutation of base metals into gold but also the foundation for the inner work of spiritual enlightenment. In both the material and the spiritual realms, the alchemist seeks to purify and perfect the *prima materia*, bringing it to its highest, most refined form.

The idea of *prima materia* has its roots in ancient philosophical thought, particularly in the writings of Aristotle and the pre-Socratic philosophers, who speculated about the nature of the basic substance from which the cosmos is formed. In alchemical terms, *prima materia* is considered the primal chaos, the undifferentiated matter that existed before the creation of the universe. It is the "first matter" that holds within it all possibilities but is not yet shaped or defined. This concept was deeply influential in alchemy, as it implied that everything in the material world could be traced back to a single source and that this source could be transformed and elevated through the alchemical process.

For the alchemist, the process of working with *prima materia* is both a physical and spiritual journey. In physical alchemy, the *prima materia* could be represented by a base substance, such as lead, which the alchemist would attempt to transmute into gold through a series of chemical and mystical operations. However, in spiritual alchemy, the *prima materia* represents the soul in its raw, unrefined state. Just as the alchemist seeks to purify metals, so too must the individual purify their soul, stripping away the base qualities—ignorance, ego, and material attachment—in order to reveal the divine essence that lies within.

The concept of *prima materia* is often symbolized by chaotic or elemental imagery, such as the dragon, the serpent, or the formless earth. These symbols represent the primal chaos from which order and creation emerge. In many alchemical texts, the *prima materia* is depicted as dark, heavy, and impure, symbolizing the base state of the soul before it undergoes the transformative process of alchemy. This darkness, however, also contains the potential for light and perfection, echoing the alchemical belief that within the base and impure lies the seed of the divine. The task of the alchemist is to extract this potential and bring it to its highest form.

The process of transforming *prima materia* into its perfected state mirrors the stages of the alchemical Great Work, or *Magnum Opus*. The alchemical journey typically begins with *nigredo*, or blackening, the stage in which the *prima materia* is broken down and reduced to its most basic form. This phase represents the death of the ego, the dissolution of the material attachments and impurities that cloud the soul. In this stage, the alchemist faces the chaos and darkness of the unrefined self, a necessary step in the process of transformation. *Nigredo* is often associated with suffering, loss, and spiritual death, but it is seen as a prerequisite for the purification and enlightenment that follow.

After *nigredo*, the alchemical process moves to *albedo*, or whitening, in which the *prima materia* begins to be purified. In this phase, the alchemist experiences a spiritual rebirth, as the soul is cleansed of its impurities and begins to reflect the divine light. The chaos of the *prima materia* is transformed into order and clarity, symbolizing the alchemist's growing awareness of their divine nature. In this stage, the soul begins to shine with the purity of the divine essence, just as the alchemist's materials are purified and prepared for further refinement.

Citrinitas, or yellowing, follows *albedo* and represents the dawning of a new consciousness. This stage is often associated with the sun, symbolizing the illumination of the soul with divine wisdom and understanding. The *prima materia*, once dark and chaotic, is now infused with the light of knowledge and truth. The alchemist, having purified the material or spiritual substance, begins to integrate this wisdom into their being. This phase marks the beginning of the alchemist's mastery over the process of transformation, as they become more attuned to the divine forces at work within themselves and the universe.

The final stage of the alchemical Great Work is *rubedo*, or reddening, in which the *prima materia* is brought to its perfected state. This stage represents the culmination of the alchemical process, where the substance has been fully transformed into its highest form. In spiritual alchemy, this corresponds to the individual's attainment of spiritual enlightenment, where the soul is fully aligned with the divine. The red color of *rubedo* symbolizes life, vitality, and the union of opposites—masculine and feminine, spirit and matter—within the alchemist's soul. The *prima materia* has now been transmuted into the Philosopher's Stone, the ultimate symbol of spiritual perfection.

For the Rosicrucians, who were deeply influenced by alchemical thought, the concept of *prima materia* held profound significance. They believed that the raw, unformed potential within each individual could be shaped and refined through a process of spiritual alchemy, leading to the realization of divine wisdom and the transformation of the world. In this sense, *prima materia* was not just a physical substance but a symbol of the soul's potential for growth and enlightenment. By engaging with the alchemical process, the Rosicrucians sought to unlock this potential, transforming the chaos of the material world into a reflection of the divine order.

In both alchemical and Rosicrucian traditions, *prima materia* represents the starting point for a journey of transformation, a journey that leads from chaos to order, from darkness to light, and from base material to spiritual perfection. The alchemist's work with the *prima materia* serves as a metaphor for the inner work that each individual must undertake in order to achieve harmony with the divine and realize their true potential. Through this process of purification and transformation, the *prima materia* becomes a sacred essence, the key to unlocking the mysteries of the cosmos and the self.

Chapter 5: The Four Elements: Earth, Water, Air, and Fire in the Rosicrucian Tradition

The four classical elements—earth, water, air, and fire—have long been central to mystical and philosophical traditions, playing a significant role in both alchemical and Rosicrucian thought. These elements were not merely understood as physical substances but as symbols of the deeper, spiritual forces that shape both the cosmos and the individual. In the Rosicrucian tradition, the elements serve as metaphors for the different aspects of the human psyche and the stages of spiritual transformation. Each element corresponds to particular qualities, processes, and stages of growth, all of which are crucial for achieving balance and enlightenment. The Rosicrucians saw the mastery and understanding of these elements as essential steps in the alchemical quest for spiritual perfection.

Earth, the densest of the four elements, represents the material world, stability, and the grounding of the self. It is associated with the body and the physical plane, where human existence is rooted. In the Rosicrucian tradition, earth symbolizes the beginning of the spiritual journey, where the individual is tied to the material world and the base desires of the ego. This element is also linked to the concept of *prima materia*, the raw substance from which all things originate. The alchemical process of transformation begins with earth, as the seeker must confront their attachment to the physical and learn to transcend the limitations of the material world. Earth is also seen as a stabilizing force, providing the foundation upon which higher spiritual work can be built. In the process of inner transformation, the qualities of earth—patience, perseverance, and structure—are necessary to cultivate the discipline required for spiritual growth.

Water, the second element, represents emotion, intuition, and the flow of life. In alchemical symbolism, water is linked to purification and the dissolving of impurities, both physical and spiritual. It is the element that washes away the ego's illusions, allowing the individual to begin the process of inner cleansing. For the Rosicrucians, water symbolizes the fluid and ever-changing nature of the human psyche, the realm of emotions, and the subconscious mind. Water also represents the connection to the divine, as it is often seen as a medium through which spiritual insight flows. In the alchemical process, water corresponds to the phase of *albedo*, or whitening, where the soul is cleansed and made pure. It is through water's reflective quality that the individual gains clarity, seeing beyond the distortions of the ego and beginning to perceive the deeper truths of existence. The fluidity of water also represents adaptability, the ability to move and change as part of the spiritual journey.

Air, the element of intellect, thought, and communication, is associated with the mind and the capacity for insight and understanding. In Rosicrucianism, air symbolizes the breath of life, the spirit that animates the body and connects the individual to the divine. It represents the intellect's ability to rise above the mundane and grasp higher truths, making air the element of inspiration and revelation. The Rosicrucians viewed air as the medium through which divine knowledge could be communicated, a symbol of the mind's potential to transcend earthly limitations. Air is also linked to the concept of the spirit or *anima*, the vital force that animates all living things. In the alchemical process, air is associated with *citrinitas*, the yellowing stage where the seeker begins to integrate intellectual and spiritual knowledge. It is through the element of air that the individual gains the understanding necessary to move forward on the path of enlightenment.

Fire, the most dynamic of the four elements, represents transformation, energy, and the will. It is the element of creation and destruction, embodying both the spark of life and the force of purification. In Rosicrucian thought, fire symbolizes the divine will, the force that drives the process of spiritual transmutation. Fire is associated with the passions, desires, and the energy needed to overcome obstacles on the spiritual path. It is the element that consumes impurities, burning away the dross of the ego and illuminating the soul. Fire is also the symbol of enlightenment, the flame of wisdom that guides the seeker through the darkness of ignorance. In alchemy, fire is the driving force behind the Great Work, representing the final stage of transformation, *rubedo*, where the alchemist achieves spiritual perfection. For the Rosicrucians, fire is both a destructive and creative force, essential for the process of rebirth and renewal. It is through the fire of transformation that the individual is able to transcend the lower self and unite with the divine.

The Rosicrucians understood the four elements not as separate, static forces but as dynamic principles that interact with and balance one another. Each element represents a different aspect of the individual and the cosmos, and it is only through the harmonious integration of all four that true spiritual enlightenment can be achieved. The alchemical process, central to Rosicrucian practice, is essentially the refinement and balancing of these elemental forces within the self. The elements also correspond to different stages in the Great Work of alchemy, with earth representing the foundation of the physical world, water symbolizing purification, air corresponding to intellectual and spiritual insight, and fire driving the final transformation.

The balance between these elements is key to understanding Rosicrucian philosophy. Just as the natural world operates in harmony with these forces, so too must the individual seek to harmonize the elements within themselves. Earth provides the grounding and stability needed to pursue higher spiritual knowledge. Water cleanses and purifies, allowing the seeker to shed the ego's illusions. Air elevates the mind, enabling the pursuit of divine wisdom. Fire ignites the will, driving the seeker to complete the process of transformation. Together, these elements form the foundation of the Rosicrucian quest for enlightenment and spiritual mastery.

Chapter 6: The Alchemical Marriage: The Union of Opposites

The Alchemical Marriage, often referred to as the *Hieros Gamos* or "sacred union," is one of the most profound symbols in alchemical and esoteric traditions, representing the union of opposites and the integration of dualities within the self. This mystical concept is at the heart of both spiritual alchemy and Rosicrucian thought, where the process of merging opposing forces is seen as essential for achieving inner harmony and spiritual transformation. The Alchemical Marriage is not merely about the physical joining of male and female but a metaphorical and spiritual union that takes place within the individual. It symbolizes the reconciliation of polarities, such as masculine and feminine, light and dark, spirit and matter, which, when integrated, lead to a higher state of consciousness and the perfection of the soul.

In alchemical texts, the Alchemical Marriage is often depicted through the symbolic imagery of a king and queen, representing the masculine and feminine principles, coming together to create the "Philosophical Child" or "Divine Androgyne," a symbol of wholeness and spiritual completion. This union reflects the belief that the alchemist must balance the active, penetrating energy of the masculine with the receptive, nurturing energy of the feminine to achieve the Great Work, or *Magnum Opus*. In the Rosicrucian tradition, the

Alchemical Marriage also represents the synthesis of the material and spiritual realms, where the seeker harmonizes the physical body and the higher soul to ascend to a state of divine wisdom and enlightenment.

The masculine and feminine principles in alchemy correspond to the sun and moon, often depicted as royal figures in alchemical manuscripts. The sun, associated with the masculine, represents consciousness, intellect, and the active force that initiates change. The moon, representing the feminine, symbolizes intuition, the subconscious, and the passive force that receives and reflects light. These two principles are seen as complementary and interdependent, requiring each other to achieve balance. The Alchemical Marriage brings these opposing forces into alignment, where they no longer function in isolation but work together to produce the "elixir of life" or the Philosopher's Stone—metaphors for spiritual perfection and immortality.

The union of opposites in the Alchemical Marriage is a reflection of a greater cosmic order, one that is echoed in the Hermetic axiom "As above, so below." This principle, central to both alchemical and Rosicrucian thought, asserts that the processes and relationships that occur in the heavens are mirrored on Earth and within the human soul. Just as the cosmos is a balance of light and dark, creation and destruction, so too must the individual harmonize the opposing forces within themselves to achieve inner equilibrium. The Alchemical

Marriage is a personal, internal process that mirrors this larger cosmic balance, teaching that enlightenment comes not from denying or suppressing one side of the duality but from the synthesis of both.

This sacred union is not just about reconciling external opposites but involves an inner alchemical process that transforms the soul. In spiritual alchemy, the stages of the *Magnum Opus*—*nigredo* (blackening), *albedo* (whitening), *citrinitas* (yellowing), and *rubedo* (reddening)—represent phases of inner purification and transformation that lead to the final union. The *nigredo* stage symbolizes the death of the ego, where the individual must confront their inner darkness and shadow aspects. *Albedo* represents the purification of the soul, a cleansing that prepares the seeker for the integration of divine wisdom. In *citrinitas*, the seeker begins to internalize spiritual truths, leading to the illumination of the soul. Finally, in *rubedo*, the union is complete, and the individual has achieved the Alchemical Marriage—the harmonious blending of spirit and matter, masculine and feminine, within themselves.

The concept of the Alchemical Marriage also has strong psychological undertones, particularly in the way it reflects the integration of the conscious and unconscious mind. Carl Jung, the Swiss psychologist, was particularly interested in the symbolic meaning of the Alchemical Marriage, seeing it as an expression of the process of individuation—the psychological journey toward self-realization and wholeness. In Jungian terms, the Alchemical Marriage represents the union of the animus (the masculine aspect of the psyche) and the anima (the feminine aspect), leading to psychological balance and completeness. This mirrors the alchemical idea that the seeker must unite the conscious, rational mind (associated with the masculine) with the unconscious, intuitive self (associated with the feminine) to achieve inner harmony and transcendence.

In Rosicrucianism, the Alchemical Marriage is also tied to the concept of the "Chymical Wedding," as described in the *Chymical Wedding of Christian Rosenkreuz*, one of the foundational Rosicrucian texts. In this allegorical tale, Christian Rosenkreuz is invited to attend a mystical wedding, a journey that represents his own process of spiritual transformation. The wedding in the story is filled with alchemical symbolism, including the union of the king and queen, which signifies the culmination of Rosenkreuz's quest for enlightenment. This allegory reflects the Rosicrucian belief that the Alchemical Marriage is not just a mystical event but a personal journey of spiritual awakening, where the seeker must harmonize the opposites within themselves to achieve unity with the divine.

The Alchemical Marriage also serves as a reminder of the importance of balance in all aspects of life. For the alchemist, achieving this sacred union means embracing both the light and the dark, the masculine and feminine, and integrating these forces into a single, unified whole.

This process is not one of conflict but of synthesis, where opposites do not cancel each other out but rather complement and complete one another. In this sense, the Alchemical Marriage is both a personal and universal symbol, representing the union of dualities that exists within the individual, the cosmos, and the divine.

The imagery of the Alchemical Marriage, with its emphasis on unity and transformation, remains one of the most powerful symbols in alchemical and Rosicrucian thought. It speaks to the deep human desire for wholeness, the yearning to transcend duality and achieve a higher state of being where all aspects of the self are integrated and harmonized. The sacred union of opposites in the Alchemical Marriage is not a final destination but an ongoing process, a continual journey of balancing and reconciling the forces within, leading the seeker ever closer to spiritual perfection.

Chapter 7: Sol and Luna: The Sun and Moon as Mystical Archetypes

In alchemical and esoteric traditions, the sun and moon, often referred to as Sol and Luna, serve as powerful mystical archetypes that symbolize the dualities present within the cosmos and the human soul. These celestial bodies are not merely physical objects in the sky but are imbued with deep symbolic meaning, representing the masculine and feminine principles, the conscious and unconscious, and the dynamic forces of creation and transformation. In alchemy, Rosicrucianism, and related mystical systems, Sol and Luna are depicted as complementary forces whose union is essential for achieving spiritual enlightenment and the Great Work of alchemical transformation.

Sol, the sun, is traditionally associated with the masculine principle, representing consciousness, rationality, and the active force that brings life and energy to the world. It is the source of light, warmth, and vitality, illuminating the darkness and enabling growth. In mystical and alchemical thought, the sun symbolizes the conscious mind, the ego, and the divine spark that resides within each individual. Sol is often depicted as a king, radiant and powerful, governing the material and intellectual realms. The alchemist or spiritual seeker must harness the energy of Sol to bring clarity, order, and focus to their quest for enlightenment.

Luna, the moon, represents the feminine principle, associated with intuition, receptivity, and the mysteries of the unconscious. Unlike Sol's steady and constant light, Luna's light is reflective and cyclical, waxing and waning in phases. This reflects the moon's connection to the rhythms of nature, the tides, and the cyclical nature of human emotions and spiritual growth. In alchemy, Luna symbolizes the subconscious, the emotional world, and the spiritual depths that lie hidden beneath the surface of consciousness. Luna is often depicted as a queen, serene and mysterious, ruling over the night and the unseen realms of the psyche. The seeker must engage with the energy of Luna to access the intuitive, emotional, and spiritual aspects of their being, which are necessary for deep transformation.

The relationship between Sol and Luna in alchemical symbolism reflects the broader theme of duality and the need for integration. The sun and moon are often depicted as a divine pair, whose union leads to the creation of the "Philosophical Child," a symbol of spiritual perfection and the completion of the Great Work. This union, known as the Alchemical Marriage, represents the merging of opposites—masculine and feminine, light and dark, consciousness and unconsciousness—into a harmonious whole. In this sense, Sol and Luna are not seen as opposing forces but as complementary aspects of a greater unity. Their interplay is essential for the process of inner alchemy, where the individual seeks to balance and integrate these dual forces within themselves to achieve enlightenment.

In many alchemical texts, Sol and Luna are associated with the process of transformation that leads to the creation of the Philosopher's Stone, the ultimate symbol of spiritual and material perfection. The sun's fiery energy is linked to the purification of the soul, burning away impurities and illuminating the path to wisdom. The moon's reflective and nurturing energy supports the alchemist's journey inward, helping them to explore the deeper, hidden aspects of their psyche. Together, Sol and Luna represent the complete alchemical process, where both the active and passive, rational and intuitive, are necessary to achieve the transformation of the self.

The symbolism of Sol and Luna also extends to the body and spirit. In many esoteric traditions, the sun is associated with the spirit, or the divine spark within, while the moon is connected to the soul and the emotional body. The alchemist's task is to bring these two aspects of the self into alignment, uniting spirit and soul, so that they work in harmony toward the goal of spiritual realization. Sol's radiant energy brings the clarity and focus needed to guide the alchemist on their journey, while Luna's gentle light allows for reflection, introspection, and the nurturing of the inner world. Through the integration of these energies, the alchemist is able to transcend the limitations of the material world and ascend to a higher state of consciousness.

In the Rosicrucian tradition, Sol and Luna take on additional layers of meaning, representing the interplay between the divine masculine and feminine within the broader cosmic order. The Rosicrucians, like the alchemists, viewed the union of these forces as essential for both personal and universal transformation. Sol, as the masculine, is associated with wisdom, reason, and the active principle of creation, while Luna, as the feminine, is connected to love, intuition, and the passive, receptive principle. Together, they embody the Hermetic ideal of balance between the active and passive forces of the universe, reflecting the Rosicrucian belief in the interconnectedness of all things.

The sun and moon are also linked to the different stages of the alchemical Great Work. Sol is associated with the later stages of the process, particularly the phase of *rubedo* or reddening, where the alchemist achieves the final integration of spirit and matter, symbolized by the color red and the full brilliance of the sun. Luna, on the other hand, is associated with the earlier stages, such as *albedo* or whitening, where the soul is purified and prepared for the greater work to come. This connection between the elements of Sol and Luna and the phases of the Great Work reflects the idea that spiritual transformation is a gradual process, where both light and darkness, action and reflection, are necessary for growth.

The cyclical nature of Luna's phases also serves as a reminder of the recurring nature of spiritual development. Just as the moon waxes and wanes, so too does the seeker's journey through moments of clarity and darkness, growth and retreat. Luna's cycles mirror the rhythms of nature and human life, reminding the alchemist that spiritual progress is not linear but requires patience, reflection, and adaptability. In contrast, Sol's steady light provides a sense of constancy and purpose, guiding the alchemist through the inevitable challenges and changes of the spiritual path.

Through the archetypes of Sol and Luna, the alchemist is reminded of the importance of balance and integration in their quest for enlightenment. The sun and moon, as symbols of the masculine and feminine, conscious and unconscious, and active and receptive forces, offer a profound guide for understanding the dualities that shape both the cosmos and the self. By uniting these energies within, the alchemist follows the path toward spiritual transformation, seeking to create harmony between the opposites and unlock the divine wisdom that resides at the core of their being.

Chapter 8: The Transmutation Process: Physical and Spiritual Transformation

The transmutation process in alchemy is most famously associated with the transformation of base metals into gold, but its deeper significance lies in its role as a metaphor for spiritual transformation. In the esoteric traditions of alchemy and Rosicrucianism, transmutation is not just a physical process but also a profound spiritual journey. It represents the purification and elevation of the human soul, mirroring the steps an alchemist takes in the laboratory to refine substances. This dual approach—physical and spiritual—shows how the outer work of transforming metals serves as a symbolic reflection of the inner work of transforming the self. The process of transmutation involves multiple stages, each one aligned with the spiritual purification of the soul, and is central to the alchemist's quest for enlightenment and self-realization.

The first stage of transmutation, often referred to as *nigredo*, or blackening, is where the process begins, both physically and spiritually. In the physical sense, this stage represents the decomposition and breaking down of the base material, reducing it to its most essential form. This destruction is necessary to strip away impurities, just as the alchemist must strip away the ego and material attachments that cloud the spirit. Spiritually, *nigredo* signifies the dark night of the soul, a phase where the individual confronts their own inner darkness and chaos. It is a period of suffering, confusion, and dissolution, but one that is essential for growth. By facing the shadow aspects of the self, the seeker clears the way for the transformation that follows, laying the foundation for deeper spiritual work.

Once the base material has been broken down, the next stage is *albedo*, or whitening, which represents the purification of both the physical substance and the soul. In alchemy, this stage is often symbolized by the washing of the material to remove all impurities, leaving behind a clean, purified substance. On a spiritual level, *albedo* is associated with enlightenment and clarity, where the seeker begins to experience a sense of renewal and spiritual rebirth. The darkness of the *nigredo* phase gives way to light, as the individual gains insight into their true nature and begins to align more closely with the divine. This stage is also linked to the development of virtues such as humility, compassion, and purity of heart, all of which are necessary for the next phase of transformation.

The third stage of transmutation is *citrinitas*, or yellowing, which marks the beginning of the final transformation into spiritual and material gold. In the physical alchemical process, *citrinitas* is the stage where the purified substance begins to take on new properties, becoming more refined and closer to its ultimate goal of perfection. Spiritually, *citrinitas* represents the dawning of higher consciousness and wisdom. The seeker, having gone through purification, now begins to internalize the divine truths they have encountered. The mind becomes illuminated, and the individual begins to see the world with a new perspective, one that is guided by spiritual knowledge rather than material concerns. This stage reflects the transition from the intellectual understanding of spiritual principles to the deeper, experiential wisdom that comes from living those truths.

The final stage of the transmutation process is *rubedo*, or reddening, where the material is transmuted into gold, and the spiritual seeker achieves union with the divine. In alchemy, this stage is the culmination of the Great Work, where the base substance has been fully transformed into its highest and most perfect form. Spiritually, *rubedo* signifies the attainment of enlightenment, where the individual has fully integrated the physical and spiritual aspects of their being. The alchemist, now purified and enlightened, has reached the pinnacle of their journey, where the dualities of the material and spiritual worlds are reconciled, and the seeker experiences a sense of oneness with the divine. This final stage is often depicted as the creation of the Philosopher's Stone, a symbol of both material wealth and spiritual immortality.

Throughout the transmutation process, the alchemist must engage in both physical and spiritual practices to achieve the desired transformation. In the physical realm, this involves careful observation, experimentation, and patience, as the alchemist works with various materials and substances to refine them into their purest form. Each step of the physical process serves as a mirror for the inner work of self-purification and spiritual growth. The alchemist must also cultivate inner virtues such as perseverance, discipline, and humility, recognizing that the outer transformation of matter is only possible when accompanied by the inner transformation of the self.

The connection between the physical and spiritual aspects of transmutation is rooted in the alchemical belief that the material world is a reflection of the spiritual world, and that by working with matter, the alchemist can gain insight into the workings of the soul. This belief is expressed in the famous Hermetic axiom "As above, so below," which teaches that the processes of nature are mirrored in the human spirit. By engaging in the physical act of transmutation, the alchemist not only transforms base metals into gold but also refines and elevates their own soul, achieving a state of spiritual perfection.

The transmutation process in alchemy is thus a complex and multi-layered journey that involves both physical experimentation and deep spiritual work. Through the stages of *nigredo*, *albedo*, *citrinitas*, and *rubedo*, the alchemist seeks to transform the raw material of both the physical world and the self into their highest and most perfected state. This process reflects the core belief of alchemical and esoteric traditions: that the physical and spiritual realms are intimately connected, and that by mastering the principles of transmutation, the individual can achieve both material and spiritual enlightenment.

Chapter 9: Alchemical Symbols in Rosicrucian Manuscripts

Alchemical symbols play a pivotal role in Rosicrucian manuscripts, serving as a secret language through which complex spiritual and philosophical ideas are conveyed. These symbols, often drawn from traditional alchemy, reflect both the physical and spiritual aspects of the Great Work, or *Magnum Opus*, that defines the Rosicrucian quest for enlightenment. In Rosicrucianism, as in alchemy, symbols are not merely decorative or illustrative; they carry profound meaning, inviting the initiate to contemplate the mysteries of transformation, purification, and the union of opposites. Each symbol encapsulates a stage of spiritual development or a fundamental truth about the nature of the universe, urging the seeker to decode its hidden meanings and apply its lessons to their inner journey.

One of the most prominent alchemical symbols in Rosicrucian manuscripts is the rose itself, often intertwined with the cross. The rose symbolizes beauty, purity, and the unfolding of divine knowledge, while the cross represents the material world, suffering, and the process of death and rebirth. Together, the rose and the cross encapsulate the core Rosicrucian belief in the necessity of personal sacrifice and transformation to achieve spiritual awakening. The rose's petals, often depicted in stages of unfolding, represent the gradual revelation of higher truths as the seeker progresses on their spiritual path. This symbolism mirrors the alchemical idea of purification, where the soul, like a base metal, must undergo stages of refinement to reveal its divine essence.

The ouroboros, another important symbol in both alchemy and Rosicrucianism, is the image of a serpent or dragon devouring its own tail. This symbol represents the cyclical nature of life, death, and rebirth, as well as the concept of eternity and the unity of all things. In Rosicrucian thought, the ouroboros symbolizes the infinite process of spiritual growth, where the end of one cycle is the beginning of another. This reflects the alchemical principle that spiritual enlightenment is not a final state but a continuous process of transformation. The ouroboros also emphasizes the importance of balance, suggesting that creation and destruction, life and death, are intertwined forces that must be harmonized within the individual.

The symbol of the Philosopher's Stone, though often associated with the literal alchemical goal of transmuting base metals into gold, holds a far deeper significance in Rosicrucian manuscripts. The Philosopher's Stone represents the ultimate goal of spiritual perfection, where the individual achieves the unity of body, mind, and spirit. In Rosicrucian texts, the Philosopher's Stone is sometimes depicted as a radiant, geometric shape or a luminous object, symbolizing the enlightenment that comes from the successful completion of the Great Work. The Stone is not merely an object but a state of being, where the individual has transcended the limitations of the material world and aligned themselves with divine will. This concept is closely linked to the Rosicrucian ideal of the "invisible college," where members of the brotherhood are initiated into the mysteries of the universe and gain access to the hidden truths that govern existence.

Alchemical symbols in Rosicrucian manuscripts also include references to the four classical elements: earth, water, air, and fire. These elements, which were believed to constitute all matter in the physical world, also represent the various stages of spiritual development. Earth, symbolizing stability and grounding, corresponds to the base state of the soul, where the individual is tied to the material world. Water, symbolizing purification and emotion, represents the phase of cleansing the soul, washing away impurities to prepare for enlightenment. Air, representing intellect and spirit, corresponds to the illumination that comes with the acquisition of divine knowledge. Fire, symbolizing transformation and willpower, represents the final stage of spiritual transmutation, where the soul is purified by the divine flame and reborn into a higher state of consciousness.

The alchemical symbol of the sun (Sol) and moon (Luna) is another powerful image found in Rosicrucian manuscripts, representing the masculine and feminine principles and the union of opposites. Sol, associated with the active, rational, and conscious aspects of the self, is often depicted as a radiant king, while Luna, associated with the passive, intuitive, and subconscious, is represented as a serene queen. The union of Sol and Luna, also known as the "Alchemical Marriage," symbolizes the reconciliation of these opposing forces within the individual. In alchemy, this union is the key to creating the Philosopher's Stone, and in Rosicrucian thought, it represents the process of integrating the dualities of the self to achieve spiritual wholeness.

Another recurring alchemical symbol in Rosicrucian manuscripts is the image of the dragon, which represents both the primal chaos and the potential for transformation. The dragon is often associated with the *prima materia*, the raw, unrefined substance that alchemists believed contained the potential for all creation. In Rosicrucian thought, the dragon symbolizes the untamed forces within the individual—the base instincts and unrefined emotions that must be confronted and transformed in the process of spiritual growth. The slaying of the dragon, a common theme in both alchemical and Rosicrucian allegory, represents the victory of the higher self over the lower self, where the individual conquers their baser instincts and emerges purified and enlightened.

The pelican is another symbol rich in alchemical and Rosicrucian meaning. Depicted as a bird that pierces its own breast to feed its young with its blood, the pelican symbolizes self-sacrifice, compassion, and the regeneration of life through selfless love. In Rosicrucian manuscripts, the pelican is often associated with the concept of spiritual rebirth, where the seeker must be willing to sacrifice their ego and lower desires in order to nurture their higher self. This image aligns with the alchemical idea of the dissolution of the ego, where the individual undergoes a symbolic death in order to be reborn into a more enlightened state of being.

Alchemical symbols in Rosicrucian manuscripts are not just artistic flourishes or esoteric puzzles; they are tools for contemplation and vehicles for transmitting complex spiritual truths. Each symbol encapsulates multiple layers of meaning, inviting the initiate to explore the depths of its significance and apply its wisdom to their own spiritual journey. Through the use of these symbols, the Rosicrucians communicate their belief in the possibility of human transformation, where the material and the spiritual, the seen and the unseen, are inextricably linked in the quest for enlightenment and union with the divine.

Chapter 10: The Path of Gold: The Rosicrucian Alchemist's Journey to Enlightenment

The Path of Gold, as understood by the Rosicrucian alchemist, is a journey of spiritual transformation where enlightenment is achieved through the alchemical process of purifying the soul and aligning oneself with divine principles. This journey is often described in the language of alchemy, where gold serves as a metaphor for the highest state of spiritual perfection. For the Rosicrucians, gold is not simply a material substance but a symbol of the soul's potential to reach its most refined and enlightened state. The alchemical quest for gold is thus a deeply internal process, where the individual undergoes a series of transformations that parallel the physical work of the alchemist in the laboratory.

At the heart of this journey is the concept of *prima materia*, the base or raw substance from which all alchemical transformations begin. In the Rosicrucian tradition, *prima materia* represents the unrefined aspects of the self—the ego, the attachments to the material world, and the unexamined desires that prevent the soul from realizing its divine nature. The alchemist's task is to confront this base material within themselves and begin the process of purification. This stage, often referred to as *nigredo*, or blackening, symbolizes the dissolution of the ego and the confrontation with one's inner darkness. The Rosicrucian alchemist must willingly undergo this difficult process, acknowledging and accepting their imperfections in order to prepare for the later stages of transformation.

As the alchemist moves through the stages of purification, the next phase is *albedo*, or whitening, where the soul begins to be cleansed of its impurities. In this stage, the Rosicrucian alchemist experiences the first glimmers of spiritual awakening, as the darkness of the *nigredo* phase gives way to the light of inner clarity and understanding. This phase is marked by a sense of renewal, where the soul is purified and begins to align more closely with the divine. The alchemist's journey is no longer about confronting the shadow aspects of the self but about nurturing the growing light within. It is during *albedo* that the alchemist learns to cultivate virtues such as humility, compassion, and patience, all of which are necessary for the deeper stages of transformation that lie ahead.

Following *albedo* comes *citrinitas*, or yellowing, where the alchemist's purified soul begins to shine with the light of wisdom and knowledge. In Rosicrucian teachings, this stage represents the dawning of higher consciousness, where the individual starts to perceive the deeper truths of the universe. The gold that was once hidden within the base material begins to emerge, symbolizing the increasing alignment of the soul with divine principles. *Citrinitas* is often associated with the sun, whose yellow light symbolizes illumination and the rising of consciousness. In this phase, the

Rosicrucian alchemist gains the insight needed to navigate the complexities of the spiritual path, and their understanding of the interconnectedness of all things deepens.

The final stage of the alchemical journey is *rubedo*, or reddening, where the process of transformation is completed, and the alchemist achieves spiritual perfection. In Rosicrucian thought, *rubedo* represents the culmination of the alchemist's work, where the soul has been fully purified and transformed into its highest state. This phase is symbolized by the creation of the Philosopher's Stone, a symbol of both material and spiritual gold. For the Rosicrucian alchemist, the Philosopher's Stone is not an object but a state of being, where the individual has transcended the limitations of the material world and achieved unity with the divine. *Rubedo* is the stage where the alchemist fully realizes their potential, having integrated both the masculine and feminine aspects of the self, the light and the dark, the conscious and the unconscious.

The journey along the Path of Gold is not solely about the individual's transformation but also about their role in the greater cosmic order. For the Rosicrucians, the alchemist's enlightenment is not an end in itself but a means to bring about the reformation of society and the world. The Rosicrucian alchemist, having achieved spiritual gold, is charged with using their knowledge and wisdom to uplift humanity, working in harmony with the divine to help others on their own paths of transformation. This reflects the broader Rosicrucian mission of integrating spiritual wisdom with practical, worldly action, where enlightenment is seen not as a retreat from the material world but as a way of engaging with it in a more meaningful and purposeful way.

Throughout this journey, the Rosicrucian alchemist is guided by the alchemical symbols that map out the stages of transformation. The four classical elements—earth, water, air, and fire—play a crucial role in this process, each representing a different aspect of the alchemist's journey. Earth, associated with the material world, represents the grounding of the self and the beginning of the spiritual quest. Water, symbolizing purification and emotion, reflects the cleansing of the soul. Air, representing intellect and spirit, is associated with the enlightenment that comes from divine knowledge. Fire, the element of transformation and willpower, represents the final stage of spiritual transmutation, where the soul is purified by the divine flame and reborn into a higher state of consciousness.

In Rosicrucian teachings, the journey along the Path of Gold is also marked by the reconciliation of opposites. The alchemical concept of the union of Sol and Luna, the sun and the moon, symbolizes the merging of masculine and feminine energies, the active and the receptive, the conscious and the subconscious. The alchemist must bring these opposing forces into balance, recognizing that spiritual transformation requires the integration of dualities. This union is often referred to as the Alchemical Marriage, where the alchemist achieves wholeness by harmonizing the polarities within themselves. This sacred union is essential for the final transmutation, where the alchemist becomes a living embodiment of the divine, radiating the light of spiritual gold into the world.

The Path of Gold, as understood in the Rosicrucian tradition, is a journey of continuous transformation, where the alchemist refines both the material and spiritual aspects of themselves in pursuit of enlightenment. This path requires discipline, self-reflection, and a deep commitment to inner growth, but it also promises the ultimate reward: the realization of one's divine potential and the attainment of spiritual gold. For the Rosicrucian alchemist, this journey is both deeply personal and cosmically significant, as the transmutation of the self mirrors the greater alchemical process that governs the entire universe.

BOOK 3
THE PHILOSOPHY OF THE ROSY CROSS:
ENLIGHTENMENT AND INNER TRANSFORMATION
SAMUEL SHEPHERD

Chapter 1: The Rosicrucian Worldview: Mysticism, Science, and Spirituality

The Rosicrucian worldview is a unique synthesis of mysticism, science, and spirituality, blending ancient wisdom with a progressive understanding of the universe. This fusion of thought is evident in the Rosicrucian Order's philosophy, which emphasizes the pursuit of knowledge not only as an intellectual endeavor but as a means to achieve spiritual enlightenment. Central to this worldview is the belief that the material and spiritual realms are interconnected, and that the mysteries of the universe can be unlocked through a combination of scientific inquiry, mystical experience, and spiritual practice. In this sense, Rosicrucianism offers a holistic approach to understanding existence, where the quest for truth encompasses both the visible and invisible aspects of reality.

Mysticism plays a foundational role in the Rosicrucian worldview, as the order's teachings are deeply rooted in the esoteric traditions of Hermeticism, alchemy, and Gnosticism. These traditions emphasize the existence of hidden knowledge, or *gnosis*, that is accessible to those who are spiritually prepared to receive it. For the Rosicrucians, the mystical experience is a process of inner awakening, where the individual comes to realize their connection to the divine and the greater cosmos. This realization is not merely an abstract understanding but a profound, transformative experience that aligns the seeker with higher truths. Through meditation, contemplation, and ritual, the Rosicrucian adept seeks to penetrate the veil that separates the material world from the spiritual, accessing deeper layers of reality that are not visible to the physical senses.

One of the key elements of the Rosicrucian mystical tradition is the idea of the *invisible college*, a concept that refers to the hidden brotherhood of enlightened individuals who work in secret to guide humanity's spiritual evolution. This brotherhood, often described in the Rosicrucian manifestos, operates behind the scenes, using their knowledge of the natural and spiritual laws to influence the course of human history. The idea of the invisible college reflects the Rosicrucian belief that true wisdom is not for the masses but for those who are initiated into the mysteries of the universe. The members of this invisible brotherhood are seen as custodians of ancient knowledge, who work in harmony with divine forces to bring about the reformation of society and the enlightenment of individuals.

While mysticism is central to the Rosicrucian worldview, science also holds a significant place in the order's philosophy. The Rosicrucians believe that the study of the natural world is a pathway to understanding the divine. In this sense, science and spirituality are not seen as opposing forces but as complementary aspects of the quest for truth. The Rosicrucians draw on the principles of alchemy, astrology, and natural philosophy to explore the underlying patterns and forces that govern the universe. Alchemy, in particular, is not just about the physical transmutation of metals but is symbolic of the spiritual transformation of the individual. The alchemical process mirrors the journey of the soul, where the base aspects of the self are purified and refined in order to achieve spiritual perfection.

The Rosicrucian approach to science is holistic, emphasizing the interconnectedness of all things. The famous Hermetic axiom "As above, so below" encapsulates this worldview, suggesting that the microcosm of the individual reflects the macrocosm of the universe. This principle is fundamental to both Rosicrucian mysticism and science, as it implies that by studying the natural world, one can gain insight into the divine order. The Rosicrucians believe that the laws of nature are an expression of divine will, and that through scientific inquiry, one can come to understand the workings of the cosmos and their own place within it. This belief in the unity of science and spirituality influenced many intellectuals of the Renaissance and Enlightenment, who saw in the Rosicrucian tradition a model for integrating reason with mystical insight.

Spirituality, for the Rosicrucians, is not confined to religious dogma or institutionalized belief systems. Instead, it is a personal and experiential journey that each individual must undertake to discover their own connection to the divine. This journey involves the cultivation of virtues such as wisdom, compassion, and humility, which are seen as essential for spiritual growth. The Rosicrucians emphasize the importance of inner work, where the seeker must engage in self-reflection, meditation, and spiritual exercises to purify their mind and heart. This process of purification is often described in alchemical terms, where the individual undergoes a series of transformations, much like the alchemist's work in refining base metals into gold. For the Rosicrucian, enlightenment is not a sudden revelation but the result of a gradual and disciplined process of self-discovery and inner purification.

The Rosicrucian worldview also places great emphasis on the concept of universal harmony. This idea, which is rooted in both Hermetic and Neoplatonic thought, suggests that all aspects of existence are interconnected and that there is a divine order underlying the apparent chaos of the material world. The Rosicrucians believe that by aligning themselves with this cosmic order, individuals can attain a state of inner peace and enlightenment. This harmony extends beyond the individual to encompass society and the world at large, reflecting the Rosicrucian belief in the possibility of social and spiritual reformation. The Rosicrucian mission is not just about personal enlightenment but about the transformation of humanity, where individuals who have attained wisdom and understanding work together to create a more just and harmonious world.

In sum, the Rosicrucian worldview is a blend of mysticism, science, and spirituality, where the pursuit of knowledge is seen as a path to both personal and collective enlightenment. Through the study of the natural world, the practice of spiritual disciplines, and the contemplation of mystical truths, the Rosicrucian adept seeks to uncover the hidden realities of existence and align themselves with the divine. The integration of these three aspects—mysticism, science, and spirituality—forms the core of the Rosicrucian philosophy, offering a comprehensive and holistic approach to understanding the universe and the self. This worldview, which bridges the material and spiritual realms, continues to inspire those who seek a deeper connection to the mysteries of existence and a greater understanding of their place within the cosmic order.

Chapter 2: The Divine Light: The Path to Illumination

The concept of divine light holds a central place in the mystical and spiritual traditions of Rosicrucianism, serving as both a symbol and a guiding force in the path to illumination. In the Rosicrucian worldview, light is not merely a physical phenomenon but a manifestation of divine presence, the essence of truth, wisdom, and higher consciousness. This light is seen as the force that illuminates the soul, allowing the individual to transcend the darkness of ignorance and material attachment and ascend to higher realms of spiritual understanding. The path to illumination, therefore, is a journey toward the light, where the seeker gradually awakens to their own divine nature and comes into alignment with the cosmic order.

The divine light is often equated with the inner spark of divinity that resides within every individual. This inner light is a reflection of the greater divine light that pervades the universe, connecting all beings to the source of creation. In Rosicrucian teachings, the journey of spiritual enlightenment is a process of rediscovering and nurturing this inner light, which has been obscured by the ego, worldly distractions, and the illusions of the material world. Through spiritual discipline, meditation, and inner contemplation, the seeker gradually removes the veils that obscure their true nature, allowing the light within to shine forth more clearly. This process is not instantaneous but unfolds over time, as the individual deepens their understanding of themselves and their connection to the divine.

The metaphor of light and darkness is a recurring theme in Rosicrucian thought, where darkness represents ignorance, confusion, and the lower aspects of human nature, while light symbolizes knowledge, clarity, and spiritual purity. The path to illumination, therefore, is often described as a battle between light and darkness, where the individual must confront and overcome the shadow aspects of the self in order to ascend to higher levels of consciousness. This battle is not one of external conflict but an internal struggle, where the seeker must face their own fears, doubts, and weaknesses. The divine light serves as both a guide and a goal in this process, illuminating the way forward and providing the strength needed to overcome the obstacles that arise along the path.

In the Rosicrucian tradition, the light is also associated with wisdom, which is considered the highest form of knowledge. Unlike intellectual knowledge, which is based on reason and logic, wisdom is an intuitive understanding that arises from direct experience of the divine. This wisdom is often described as a kind of inner illumination, where the seeker gains insight into the hidden laws of the universe and their own place within it. The divine light, therefore, not only reveals the truth but also transforms the individual, leading to a state of inner harmony and alignment with the cosmic order. This transformation is often symbolized in alchemical terms, where the seeker undergoes a process of purification and refinement, much like the alchemist's work of transmuting base metals into gold.

The path to illumination, guided by the divine light, involves several stages of spiritual development, each marked by a deeper integration of light into the individual's being. The initial stages of the journey are often characterized by moments of insight and awakening, where the seeker begins to glimpse the truth behind the illusions of the material world. These moments of illumination are like flashes of light in the darkness, offering brief glimpses of the greater reality that lies beyond the physical senses. As the seeker progresses, these moments become more frequent and sustained, eventually leading to a state of continuous illumination, where the light of wisdom becomes a constant presence in their life.

One of the key practices in the Rosicrucian path to illumination is meditation, which is seen as a way of connecting with the inner light and attuning oneself to the divine. In meditation, the seeker quiets the mind and turns inward, focusing on the light within and allowing it to expand and fill their consciousness. This practice is not only about calming the mind but about opening the heart and soul to the presence of the divine. Through meditation, the individual becomes more receptive to the light, allowing it to flow through them and transform their inner world. This process of inner illumination is often described as a gradual awakening, where the individual becomes more aware of their true nature and their connection to the divine source.

The divine light also plays a role in the Rosicrucian understanding of healing, both physical and spiritual. In this tradition, light is seen as a healing force that can restore balance and harmony to the body, mind, and soul. The Rosicrucians believe that illness and suffering are often the result of a disconnection from the divine light, where the individual has become entangled in material concerns and lost touch with their inner essence. By reconnecting with the light, the individual can restore the natural flow of energy within their being, leading to healing and wholeness. This process of healing is not just about alleviating physical symptoms but about addressing the deeper spiritual causes of illness, bringing the individual back into alignment with the divine order.

The divine light, as understood in the Rosicrucian tradition, is also associated with the concept of the higher self, the aspect of the individual that is fully aligned with the divine. The higher self is often described as a beacon of light, guiding the individual through the challenges and trials of life. By attuning themselves to this inner guide, the seeker can navigate the complexities of the material world while staying connected to their spiritual purpose. The path to illumination, therefore, involves cultivating a relationship with the higher self, allowing its light to lead the way toward greater understanding and enlightenment.

In Rosicrucian rituals and symbols, light is frequently used as a representation of divine presence and spiritual power. Candles, for example, are often lit during ceremonies to symbolize the light of wisdom and truth. The act of lighting a candle can be seen as a metaphor for the inner process of illumination, where the individual ignites the spark of divinity within themselves and allows it to grow. Similarly, the use of symbols such as the rose and the cross in Rosicrucian teachings often incorporates the theme of light, representing the unfolding of divine knowledge and the crucifixion of the ego in the pursuit of higher truth. Through these symbols and rituals, the Rosicrucians emphasize the importance of light as a transformative force that leads to spiritual awakening and enlightenment.

Chapter 3: The Microcosm and Macrocosm: The Unity of Man and the Universe

The concept of the microcosm and macrocosm is central to the Rosicrucian and Hermetic worldview, reflecting the profound belief that there is a deep, intrinsic unity between the individual human being (the microcosm) and the larger universe (the macrocosm). This principle, rooted in ancient philosophies, holds that the same patterns, forces, and laws that govern the vast cosmos also operate within the human body and soul. Everything that exists in the external world has a corresponding aspect within the individual, and by understanding oneself, one can gain insight into the workings of the entire universe. For the Rosicrucians, this interconnectedness was not merely a philosophical idea but a spiritual truth that underpinned their quest for knowledge, healing, and enlightenment.

The axiom "As above, so below" encapsulates this relationship between the microcosm and macrocosm, suggesting that the individual is a reflection of the greater cosmos. In this view, the human being is a miniature universe, containing within themselves the same elements, forces, and energies that exist in the world around them. The Rosicrucians believed that by studying nature and the cosmos, they could learn about the human soul, and conversely, by understanding the self, they could unlock the mysteries of the universe. This holistic approach to knowledge emphasized the unity of all things and rejected the idea that the material and spiritual worlds were separate or opposed. Instead, the material world was seen as a reflection of the divine order, and human beings, as microcosms, were viewed as integral parts of this cosmic system.

In the Rosicrucian tradition, the four classical elements—earth, water, air, and fire—serve as a symbolic link between the microcosm and macrocosm. These elements were believed to constitute not only the physical universe but also the human body and soul. Earth, representing stability and structure, corresponds to the physical body and the material aspect of existence. Water, symbolizing emotion and intuition, is associated with the soul and the fluid nature of human consciousness. Air, representing intellect and thought, corresponds to the mind and the ability to reason and comprehend higher truths. Fire, symbolizing willpower and transformation, reflects the divine spark within the individual, the spiritual force that drives personal growth and enlightenment. By working to balance these elements within themselves, the Rosicrucian adept sought to bring harmony to both their inner world and their relationship with the cosmos.

The relationship between the microcosm and macrocosm is also central to the Rosicrucian understanding of health and healing. In this view, illness and imbalance within the body are seen as a reflection of disharmony in the individual's connection to the larger forces of the universe. The Rosicrucians believed that just as the elements of the universe are governed by divine laws, so too is the human body, and that by restoring harmony within the microcosm, healing could be achieved. This belief in the unity of man and the universe informed their approach to medicine and natural philosophy, where the study of astrology, alchemy, and the natural world was seen as a means of understanding both the physical and spiritual causes of illness. The alignment of the stars and planets, for example, was thought to have a direct influence on human health, reflecting the idea that the macrocosmic forces of the cosmos could manifest in the microcosmic body.

The connection between the microcosm and macrocosm also extends to the Rosicrucian understanding of the soul's journey toward enlightenment. Just as the cosmos is seen as a dynamic, evolving system, the individual is viewed as being on a path of continual growth and transformation. The stages of the alchemical Great Work—*nigredo* (blackening), *albedo* (whitening), *citrinitas* (yellowing), and *rubedo* (reddening)—are not only stages of physical transmutation but also stages of spiritual development, mirroring the processes that occur in the greater universe. In this way, the alchemical transformation of base metals into gold serves as a metaphor for the purification and perfection of the human soul. The Rosicrucian adept, by aligning themselves with the natural rhythms and laws of the universe, could achieve a state of spiritual gold, reflecting the divine perfection that exists both within themselves and in the cosmos.

Astrology, a key element of both Rosicrucian and Hermetic thought, further illustrates the relationship between the microcosm and macrocosm. The movements of the stars and planets were believed to mirror the internal processes of the individual, and the Rosicrucians studied the heavens to gain insight into human destiny and spiritual development. Each planet and star was thought to influence different aspects of the human soul, and by understanding these celestial influences, the adept could better navigate their own spiritual path. This belief in the correspondence between the heavens and the human soul reinforced the idea that the individual is deeply connected to the larger forces of the universe, and that by studying the macrocosm, they could unlock the mysteries of their own inner world.

The Rosicrucian understanding of the microcosm and macrocosm also carries a moral dimension, emphasizing the responsibility of the individual to live in harmony with the greater cosmos. Just as the universe is governed by laws of balance and order, the individual is called to cultivate virtues such as wisdom, compassion, and humility, aligning themselves with the divine principles that sustain the cosmos. In this way, the path to enlightenment is not just a personal journey but a cosmic one, where the individual's inner transformation contributes to the harmony of the entire universe. The

Rosicrucian adept, by purifying their own soul, plays a role in the greater cosmic order, reflecting the belief that the health and balance of the universe depend on the alignment of its individual parts.

Through the principle of the microcosm and macrocosm, the Rosicrucians emphasize the interconnectedness of all things, where the individual is both a reflection of the universe and an active participant in its ongoing creation. This worldview offers a holistic approach to understanding existence, where the study of the natural world, the practice of spiritual discipline, and the cultivation of inner harmony are all essential steps on the path to enlightenment. By recognizing their connection to the cosmos, the Rosicrucian adept embarks on a journey of self-discovery and transformation, where the unity of man and the universe becomes both a guiding principle and a source of profound spiritual insight.

Chapter 4: The Rose and the Cross: Symbols of Inner Transformation

The rose and the cross are two of the most significant symbols in Rosicrucianism, each carrying profound meanings related to the process of inner transformation and spiritual awakening. Together, these symbols form the emblem of the Rosicrucian Order, representing the journey of the soul from ignorance and suffering toward enlightenment and divine wisdom. The rose, with its delicate beauty and intricate layers, symbolizes the unfolding of spiritual knowledge, the blossoming of the soul, and the hidden mysteries of the universe that reveal themselves to the seeker. The cross, on the other hand, stands as a symbol of material existence, the trials of earthly life, and the process of death and rebirth that the individual must undergo to achieve higher states of consciousness. The union of these two symbols encapsulates the Rosicrucian belief in the necessity of both suffering and enlightenment on the path to spiritual transformation.

The rose has long been associated with mysticism, beauty, and divine love, and in Rosicrucian teachings, it serves as a symbol of the soul's potential for growth and enlightenment. The rose's petals, which unfold gradually, represent the stages of spiritual development, where the individual moves from a state of ignorance and darkness toward clarity and understanding. The center of the rose, often hidden and protected by its outer petals, symbolizes the innermost mysteries of existence—the divine truths that can only be revealed through inner contemplation and spiritual practice. The seeker, like the rose, must unfold layer by layer, shedding the illusions of the material world in order to reach the core of their being, where the divine essence resides.

The symbolism of the rose is also closely tied to the alchemical process of transformation, where the soul, like the base metals of alchemy, undergoes a series of purifications and refinements to reveal its true, divine nature. The different stages of the rose's bloom mirror the stages of the alchemical Great Work—*nigredo* (blackening), *albedo* (whitening), *citrinitas* (yellowing), and *rubedo* (reddening)—each representing a phase of spiritual purification and enlightenment. In this way, the rose becomes not only a symbol of beauty and divine love but also a representation of the soul's journey through the trials of transformation toward the ultimate goal of spiritual perfection.

The cross, a universal symbol of suffering, sacrifice, and resurrection, complements the symbolism of the rose by representing the material and earthly aspects of the individual's journey. The cross in Rosicrucian symbolism stands as a reminder of the trials and tribulations that are inherent in the process of spiritual growth. Just as the rose must unfold through stages of growth, the individual must confront the challenges of material existence—the ego, attachments, desires, and fears—that prevent the soul from fully blossoming. The cross, with its vertical and horizontal axes, also symbolizes the intersection of the spiritual and material worlds. The vertical axis represents the connection between the divine and the earthly, while the horizontal axis symbolizes the individual's existence in the material plane. The cross, therefore, serves as a reminder of the dual nature of human existence, where the individual must navigate both the physical and spiritual dimensions of life in order to achieve enlightenment.

In Rosicrucian teachings, the union of the rose and the cross signifies the reconciliation of opposites—the spiritual and the material, the eternal and the temporal, the divine and the human. This union is at the heart of the Rosicrucian path, where the seeker must integrate these dual aspects of existence to achieve inner harmony and spiritual transformation. The rose and the cross together form a powerful symbol of this integration, where the soul, represented by the rose, grows and flourishes through the trials and challenges represented by the cross. The thorns of the rose are also symbolic of the pain and suffering that are often necessary for growth, reminding the seeker that the path to enlightenment is not free from struggle but requires perseverance and dedication.

The rose and the cross also symbolize the process of death and rebirth, a central theme in both alchemical and Rosicrucian philosophy. The cross represents the death of the ego, the surrender of the lower self, and the dissolution of material attachments. This process of symbolic death is necessary for the soul to be reborn into a higher state of consciousness, where it can fully realize its divine potential. The rose, in this context, symbolizes the rebirth of the soul, its emergence from the darkness of ignorance into the light of spiritual understanding. The death and resurrection motif, embodied in the union of the rose and the cross, mirrors the alchemical process of transformation, where the base elements are dissolved and reconstituted into their purified form.

The Rosicrucian emblem of the rose and the cross also conveys the idea of love as a transformative force. The rose, often associated with divine love, represents the power of love to heal, uplift, and bring about spiritual awakening. The cross, traditionally associated with sacrifice, reminds the seeker that true love often requires selflessness, compassion, and the willingness to endure hardship for the sake of others. The combination of these two symbols suggests that the path to enlightenment is one that is guided by love and tempered by sacrifice, where the seeker must open their heart to both the beauty and the suffering of life in order to attain spiritual wisdom.

In Rosicrucian rituals and teachings, the rose and the cross are not only symbolic but are also used as practical tools for meditation and reflection. The initiate is often encouraged to meditate on the rose as a symbol of their own soul, contemplating its unfolding petals as a metaphor for their own spiritual growth. Similarly, the cross is used as a symbol of the trials and challenges that must be faced on the path to enlightenment, reminding the seeker that true spiritual transformation requires both inner work and the ability to navigate the difficulties of the material world. Through these practices, the Rosicrucian adept seeks to internalize the meanings of the rose and the cross, using them as guides on their journey toward spiritual mastery and self-realization.

Chapter 5: Spiritual Alchemy: The Refinement of the Soul

Spiritual alchemy is the process of refining the soul, an inner journey that mirrors the physical alchemical quest to transform base metals into gold. While physical alchemy focuses on chemical processes, spiritual alchemy transcends the material realm and centers on the transformation of the individual's consciousness. This ancient tradition, deeply rooted in both Hermeticism and Rosicrucianism, teaches that the true purpose of alchemy is the purification and perfection of the soul, where the seeker undergoes a series of trials and transformations to reach higher states of awareness and unity with the divine. The alchemical stages that guide this journey—*nigredo*, *albedo*, *citrinitas*, and *rubedo*—represent the successive phases of spiritual refinement, each contributing to the ultimate goal of enlightenment and spiritual mastery.

The first stage in spiritual alchemy, *nigredo*, or blackening, symbolizes the initial confrontation with the darker aspects of the self. This phase, often described as the "dark night of the soul," involves the dissolution of the ego and the disintegration of the false identities and attachments that have been built up over time. Just as in physical alchemy, where matter is broken down into its most basic form, the individual in the *nigredo* stage must confront their own inner chaos, fears, and shadow aspects. This is a time of deep introspection, where the seeker is forced to acknowledge the limitations and flaws of their current state of being. The darkness of *nigredo* is essential for the alchemical process, as it clears away the impurities of the soul and prepares the individual for the next stage of transformation.

After the dissolution of the *nigredo* phase, the alchemist moves into *albedo*, or whitening, a stage of purification and renewal. In this phase, the soul begins to be cleansed of its impurities, and the seeker experiences the first glimpses of spiritual awakening. *Albedo* represents the rebirth of the soul, where the individual moves from the darkness of the previous phase into the light of higher consciousness. This stage is often associated with the element of water, symbolizing the washing away of the ego and the purification of the soul. In *albedo*, the alchemist begins to cultivate virtues such as compassion, humility, and self-awareness, which are necessary for the continued progression along the spiritual path. The light of *albedo* is gentle and clarifying, offering a sense of inner peace and clarity as the individual moves closer to their true nature.

The next stage in the alchemical process is *citrinitas*, or yellowing, where the alchemist begins to internalize the spiritual insights gained during the previous stages. *Citrinitas* represents the dawning of wisdom, where the seeker starts to embody the divine knowledge they have encountered. This phase is associated with the sun, symbolizing illumination and the rising of higher consciousness. In *citrinitas*, the alchemist's soul becomes more integrated, and the individual begins to see the interconnectedness of all things. The knowledge gained in this phase is not merely intellectual but is lived and experienced on a deeper, more intuitive level. *Citrinitas* is a time of synthesis, where the seeker begins to harmonize the spiritual and material aspects of their life, preparing for the final stage of transformation. The final stage of spiritual alchemy is *rubedo*, or reddening, where the alchemist achieves the union of spirit and matter and attains the highest level of spiritual enlightenment. In this phase, the soul has been fully purified, and the individual reaches a state of wholeness and unity with the divine. *Rubedo* represents the completion of the Great Work, where the alchemist becomes the "Philosopher's Stone"—a living embodiment of spiritual perfection. In this stage, the alchemist has integrated all aspects of their being, including the masculine and feminine, the conscious and unconscious, and the spiritual and material. *Rubedo* is symbolized by the color red, representing life force, vitality, and the full expression of the individual's divine potential. At this stage, the alchemist radiates wisdom, compassion, and love, having transcended the limitations of the ego and material existence.

Throughout the process of spiritual alchemy, the alchemist must engage in practices that support the refinement of the soul. Meditation, contemplation, and inner reflection are essential tools in this process, allowing the seeker to attune to the divine light within and purify their thoughts, emotions, and actions. Just as the physical alchemist works with fire to transform metals, the spiritual alchemist uses the "fire" of discipline, perseverance, and self-awareness to burn away impurities and refine the soul. This inner fire is often seen as the divine spark that resides within each individual, guiding them toward their true nature and ultimate purpose.

In spiritual alchemy, the transformation of the soul is not an isolated endeavor but is deeply interconnected with the cosmos. The alchemist understands that the same principles that govern the transformation of matter also apply to the transformation of consciousness. The Hermetic axiom "As above, so below" reflects this understanding, suggesting that the processes of spiritual alchemy mirror the greater forces at work in the universe. By aligning themselves with these universal laws, the alchemist can tap into the hidden forces of creation and facilitate their own spiritual evolution. This holistic approach to transformation emphasizes the unity of all things, where the individual's inner work contributes to the greater harmony of the cosmos.

The ultimate goal of spiritual alchemy is the realization of the divine self, where the individual transcends the limitations of the ego and material existence to become one with the divine. This process is not merely about personal enlightenment but about contributing to the spiritual evolution of humanity and the world. The alchemist, having refined their soul through the stages of transformation, becomes a vessel for divine wisdom and compassion, using their knowledge to uplift others and bring about positive change. Spiritual alchemy, therefore, is both a personal journey of inner transformation and a path of service to the greater good, where the refinement of the soul leads to the realization of one's divine purpose and the fulfillment of the Great Work.

Chapter 6: The Sacred Geometry of the Rosy Cross: Unlocking Universal Laws

The sacred geometry of the Rosy Cross is deeply embedded in the Rosicrucian tradition, symbolizing the hidden laws of the universe and the intricate relationship between the material and spiritual worlds. Geometry, in this context, is not merely a mathematical discipline but a reflection of divine order, embodying the fundamental patterns through which the cosmos is structured. The Rosy Cross itself, an emblem combining the rose and the cross, incorporates elements of sacred geometry to convey profound truths about creation, transformation, and spiritual enlightenment. For the Rosicrucian adept, understanding the sacred geometry of the Rosy Cross is key to unlocking the universal laws that govern both the physical world and the inner dimensions of the soul.

The cross, at the heart of the Rosy Cross symbol, is one of the most ancient geometric shapes, representing the intersection of the spiritual and material planes. Its vertical axis, pointing toward the heavens, symbolizes the divine realm and the higher spiritual aspirations of the soul. The horizontal axis, stretching across the material world, represents the plane of earthly existence and the physical realities that define human life. Together, these two axes form a cross, symbolizing the union of opposites—the meeting point between the finite and the infinite, the mortal and the eternal. The Rosicrucians believed that this intersection was where the transformative process of spiritual alchemy takes place, where the individual must balance the demands of the physical world with the higher calling of spiritual evolution.

Superimposed on the cross is the rose, which adds another layer of symbolic meaning through its connection to sacred geometry. The rose's spiral structure, often seen as a perfect expression of the golden ratio, represents growth, expansion, and the unfolding of higher consciousness. The geometry of the rose reflects the principle of harmony and proportion, which is central to the Rosicrucian understanding of the universe. Just as the petals of a rose unfold according to precise geometric patterns, so too does the soul expand and blossom as it moves through the stages of spiritual development. The rose's symmetrical form, often depicted with five petals or multiples thereof, also corresponds to the pentagram, a symbol of humanity and the microcosm, further reinforcing the idea that the human being is a reflection of the larger cosmic order.

The geometry of the Rosy Cross is also intimately connected to the Hermetic principle of "As above, so below," which suggests that the same laws governing the heavens also apply to the Earth and to the individual soul. The cross, with its intersection of vertical and horizontal planes, serves as a geometric representation of this principle, symbolizing the alignment between the microcosm and macrocosm. In this view, the individual is a reflection of the universe, and by understanding the geometric patterns that shape both the cosmos and the self, the seeker can gain insight into the underlying laws of creation. Sacred geometry, in this sense, becomes a tool for decoding the mysteries of existence, revealing the hidden order that binds all things together in a harmonious whole.

In Rosicrucian thought, the sacred geometry of the Rosy Cross also relates to the process of spiritual transformation, where the individual moves from a state of ignorance and fragmentation to one of unity and enlightenment. The geometric perfection of the cross and the rose serves as a model for the alchemical process of refinement, where the soul, like a base substance, is purified and brought into alignment with divine principles. This process is mirrored in the structure of the Rosy Cross, where the precise proportions of the cross and the harmonious unfolding of the rose represent the stages of spiritual development. As the seeker contemplates the geometry of the Rosy Cross, they are reminded of the need for balance and harmony in their own life, where the different aspects of their being—mind, body, and spirit—must be integrated into a unified whole.

The sacred geometry of the Rosy Cross also has profound implications for the Rosicrucian understanding of the universe as a living organism, governed by the same principles of proportion, harmony, and balance that are reflected in the geometry of the cross and the rose. The Rosicrucians viewed the universe as a vast, interconnected system, where every part reflects the whole and every whole is composed of parts that follow the same geometric laws. This holistic worldview is central to their belief in the unity of all things, where the physical and spiritual realms are not separate but are intertwined in a dynamic, evolving process. By studying the geometry of the Rosy Cross, the Rosicrucian adept learns to see the patterns of creation in all things, from the movement of the stars to the structure of the human soul.

The geometric proportions of the Rosy Cross also relate to the concept of the *quadrivium*, the four liberal arts of arithmetic, geometry, music, and astronomy, which were considered essential for understanding the natural and divine laws of the universe. In Rosicrucian thought, geometry is the key to unlocking these laws, as it provides the structure upon which all other knowledge is built. The cross, with its four equal arms, represents the balance between these four disciplines, while the rose, with its harmonious proportions, symbolizes the integration of these disciplines into a unified understanding of the cosmos. This reflects the Rosicrucian belief in the interconnectedness of all fields of knowledge, where the study of geometry is not just an intellectual exercise but a path to spiritual insight and enlightenment.

The sacred geometry of the Rosy Cross also plays a role in the rituals and meditative practices of the Rosicrucians, where the contemplation of geometric symbols is used as a means of aligning the individual with the cosmic order. By meditating on the precise proportions and harmonious structure of the Rosy Cross, the seeker attunes themselves to the divine laws that govern both the physical and spiritual realms. This practice is seen as a way of accessing higher states of consciousness, where the individual transcends the limitations of the material world and enters into a deeper understanding of the unity of all things. Through this process, the Rosicrucian adept not only gains insight into the mysteries of the universe but also experiences the transformative power of sacred geometry in their own spiritual journey.

Chapter 7: Inner Silence and Meditation: Keys to Rosicrucian Wisdom

Inner silence and meditation are essential practices within the Rosicrucian tradition, regarded as the primary keys to unlocking deeper wisdom and spiritual transformation. For the Rosicrucian seeker, the cultivation of inner silence is not merely the absence of external noise but the quieting of the mind, emotions, and distractions of the material world to allow for a profound connection with the inner self and the divine. Meditation is the vehicle through which this silence is achieved, providing a method for turning inward and accessing the hidden realms of knowledge that lie within. In the Rosicrucian worldview, the mind, when still and receptive, becomes a gateway to higher planes of consciousness, where the seeker can commune with the wisdom of the cosmos and gain insights that are inaccessible through ordinary, conscious thought.

Inner silence, in this context, is the state in which the individual becomes attuned to the subtler aspects of their being and to the spiritual energies that pervade the universe. Rosicrucians believe that the constant noise of everyday life, as well as the chatter of the untrained mind, creates a barrier between the seeker and the higher truths they seek to understand. Achieving inner silence requires the practitioner to quiet the restless thoughts and emotions that dominate the surface level of awareness. In this state of mental stillness, the Rosicrucian adept can access a deeper level of consciousness, where the intuitive mind becomes more active and where spiritual truths can be perceived directly. This silence is not an empty void but a space of immense potential, where the subtle voice of the soul and the higher self can be heard.

Meditation, as practiced in the Rosicrucian tradition, is the disciplined method for entering into this state of inner silence. The purpose of meditation is to create a bridge between the conscious mind and the deeper levels of the psyche, allowing the individual to bypass the distractions of the material world and connect with the inner source of wisdom. Rosicrucian meditation often involves focused attention on specific symbols, thoughts, or states of being, such as the contemplation of sacred geometry, the Rosy Cross, or the light of the inner self. By focusing the mind on these symbols, the seeker gradually quiets the surface-level thoughts and opens themselves to the higher vibrations of spiritual energy. Meditation is not simply a practice of relaxation but an active process of aligning the self with the divine order, bringing the mind, body, and spirit into harmony.

Through meditation, the Rosicrucian practitioner learns to access deeper states of consciousness, where the distinctions between the material and spiritual worlds begin to dissolve. This process of inner exploration allows the seeker to move beyond the limitations of the physical senses and intellect, entering into a realm of direct experience and intuition. In this meditative state, the individual can perceive the underlying patterns of existence, gaining insight into the laws that govern both the universe and the self. The practice of meditation is seen as a way of aligning with the cosmic order, where the individual becomes attuned to the rhythms of nature and the higher forces that shape reality. This alignment is central to the Rosicrucian pursuit of wisdom, as it allows the seeker to experience the unity of all things and to understand their place within the greater scheme of creation.

Inner silence, when combined with meditation, also serves as a means of self-purification in the Rosicrucian tradition. The act of quieting the mind is itself a process of refining the self, stripping away the layers of ego, desire, and attachment that obscure the true nature of the soul. In the silence of meditation, the seeker confronts their own inner landscape, facing the fears, doubts, and unresolved emotions that hinder spiritual growth. Through this process, the individual gradually clears away the impurities of the lower self, allowing the light of the higher self to shine through more clearly. This purification is essential for the Rosicrucian path, as it prepares the seeker to receive higher knowledge and to act as a vessel for divine wisdom.

The Rosicrucian belief in the power of inner silence and meditation is also tied to the concept of divine illumination. In the state of inner silence, the mind becomes receptive to the influx of divine light, which is often described as the source of all wisdom and understanding. This light is not perceived through the physical senses but is experienced inwardly, as a sudden realization or intuitive insight. In the stillness of meditation, the seeker becomes a conduit for this light, allowing it to penetrate the mind and soul, revealing deeper truths about the self and the universe. The experience of divine illumination is considered one of the highest goals of Rosicrucian meditation, as it represents a direct connection with the divine source of all knowledge.

Inner silence and meditation also have practical applications in the Rosicrucian way of life, guiding the individual in making decisions and navigating the challenges of the material world. By regularly practicing meditation, the Rosicrucian adept cultivates a deeper sense of inner peace and clarity, allowing them to respond to situations with greater wisdom and insight. In moments of stress or difficulty, the practitioner can return to the silence within, finding the strength and guidance they need to act in alignment with their higher purpose. This connection to inner silence is seen as a source of strength, providing the individual with a constant sense of grounding and stability, even in the face of external chaos.

Meditation and inner silence are therefore not only methods for personal enlightenment but also tools for practical living in the Rosicrucian tradition. Through these practices, the seeker is able to maintain a connection to the divine while engaging with the challenges of daily life. This balance between the inner and outer worlds is central to the Rosicrucian philosophy, where spiritual wisdom is not seen as something separate from the material world but as a guiding force that informs every aspect of existence.

Chapter 8: The Concept of Rebirth: Life, Death, and Renewal in Rosicrucian Thought

The concept of rebirth in Rosicrucian thought reflects a profound understanding of life, death, and renewal as interconnected processes that are essential to the spiritual evolution of the individual. In the Rosicrucian worldview, death is not seen as an end but as a transformation, a necessary step in the soul's journey toward higher consciousness. This idea of cyclical renewal, where death leads to rebirth, is central to the alchemical and mystical teachings of the Rosicrucian tradition. The notion of rebirth encompasses both literal and symbolic interpretations—spanning the physical cycle of life and death, as well as the metaphorical death and rebirth of the soul as it undergoes spiritual purification and enlightenment.

At its core, rebirth in Rosicrucianism is tied to the alchemical process of transformation, where the individual must shed the old, base elements of their being to make way for the refined, purified self. This process is often described using the stages of the alchemical Great Work—*nigredo* (blackening), *albedo* (whitening), *citrinitas* (yellowing), and *rubedo* (reddening)—which correspond to the spiritual stages of death, purification, illumination, and ultimate rebirth. The *nigredo* stage represents the death of the ego, the breaking down of the old self and its attachments to the material world. In this phase, the individual confronts their own inner darkness, the fears, illusions, and unfulfilled desires that keep them bound to lower states of consciousness. This symbolic death is necessary for the alchemical transformation to begin, as it clears the way for the soul to be purified and reborn.

As the individual moves through the subsequent stages of spiritual alchemy, the concept of rebirth takes on an increasingly refined and enlightened meaning. In the *albedo* stage, the soul undergoes a process of purification, where the impurities of the ego are washed away and the individual experiences a renewed sense of clarity and inner peace. This stage represents the rebirth of the purified self, where the individual is no longer governed by the illusions of the material world but is instead aligned with the higher truths of spiritual existence. The *albedo* stage is often associated with the symbol of the white rose, which represents purity, innocence, and the awakening of the soul to its true nature. In this sense, rebirth is not only the emergence of a new self but also the awakening to the higher dimensions of reality that exist beyond the physical realm.

Rebirth also plays a central role in the Rosicrucian understanding of the soul's journey through multiple lifetimes. The belief in reincarnation, or the cycle of birth, death, and rebirth, is woven into the fabric of Rosicrucian thought, where it is believed that the soul returns to the physical world in successive lifetimes to continue its process of learning, purification, and evolution. Each lifetime offers the soul new opportunities for growth and transformation, where the experiences and challenges of each incarnation contribute to the soul's ongoing refinement. In this view, death is not an end but a transition, a doorway through which the soul passes as it moves from one stage of its journey to the next. The Rosicrucians teach that through this process of reincarnation, the soul gradually ascends to higher levels of consciousness, ultimately achieving a state of spiritual perfection.

The idea of rebirth in Rosicrucianism is also deeply connected to the natural cycles of the universe, where the rhythm of life and death is mirrored in the changing seasons, the cycles of the moon, and the movements of the stars. The Rosicrucians believe that just as nature undergoes a process of death and renewal—such as the yearly cycle of winter giving way to spring—so too does the individual soul experience periods of dormancy and rebirth. This connection between the microcosm of the individual and the macrocosm of the universe reflects the Rosicrucian belief in the unity of all things, where the patterns of the cosmos are reflected in the spiritual journey of the individual. By aligning themselves with these natural cycles, the Rosicrucian adept seeks to harmonize their own process of rebirth with the greater rhythms of the universe.

In addition to the personal experience of rebirth, the concept also carries a collective dimension in Rosicrucian thought. The Rosicrucians believe that humanity as a whole is engaged in a process of spiritual evolution, where the collective consciousness of mankind is moving toward a higher state of enlightenment. Just as the individual must undergo a process of death and rebirth to achieve spiritual awakening, so too must society undergo periods of transformation and renewal. This idea is reflected in the Rosicrucian mission to reform both the individual and the world, where the knowledge and wisdom gained through personal transformation are used to uplift and enlighten humanity as a whole. The Rosicrucians see themselves as agents of this collective rebirth, working to bring about a new era of spiritual understanding and harmony.

The symbolism of the phoenix, often associated with Rosicrucian teachings, further illustrates the theme of rebirth. The phoenix, a mythical bird that is consumed by flames and then rises from its ashes, represents the eternal cycle of death and renewal. This powerful image embodies the Rosicrucian belief that through the trials of life and the fires of transformation, the soul is continually reborn into a higher state of being. The phoenix also symbolizes the immortality of the soul, the idea that the true essence of the individual cannot be destroyed but is constantly renewed through the process of death and rebirth. In this way, the concept of rebirth in Rosicrucianism transcends the physical realm and speaks to the eternal nature of the soul, which is ever-evolving and ever-renewing in its journey toward spiritual perfection.

The process of rebirth is therefore central to the Rosicrucian understanding of both individual and collective evolution, where life, death, and renewal are seen as integral parts of the spiritual path. Through this process, the individual soul is gradually purified and elevated, moving closer to its ultimate goal of union with the divine. At the same time, humanity as a whole is engaged in a collective process of rebirth, where the wisdom gained through personal transformation contributes to the spiritual evolution of the entire world. Rebirth, in this sense, is both a personal and universal process, reflecting the Rosicrucian belief in the interconnectedness of all things and the infinite potential for renewal and growth.

Chapter 9: Personal Mastery: The Quest for Enlightenment and Self-Realization

Personal mastery in the Rosicrucian tradition is a central goal of the spiritual path, representing the quest for enlightenment and self-realization. It involves the process of gaining control over the mind, emotions, and desires, allowing the individual to transcend the limitations of the ego and align with the higher aspects of their being. This quest for mastery is not simply about accumulating knowledge or intellectual understanding; it is a deep, transformative journey that requires the integration of wisdom, self-discipline, and spiritual insight. Personal mastery is the art of balancing the inner and outer worlds, achieving harmony between the spiritual and material realms, and embodying the highest principles of truth, compassion, and integrity in daily life.

The path to personal mastery begins with self-awareness, where the individual must first confront the aspects of their personality and inner world that prevent them from reaching their full potential. This process often involves facing the ego, with its attachments to material success, recognition, and pleasure, which can distract from the deeper spiritual purpose. The Rosicrucian seeker is encouraged to engage in practices such as meditation, contemplation, and self-reflection to quiet the mind and look inward. Through these practices, the individual learns to recognize the patterns of thought, behavior, and emotion that hold them back, allowing for the gradual release of these limitations.

A key component of personal mastery is the cultivation of virtues that align the individual with their higher self. In the

Rosicrucian tradition, these virtues include wisdom, humility, patience, and love. Wisdom, in this context, goes beyond mere intellectual knowledge; it is the understanding that comes from direct experience and inner insight, allowing the individual to see beyond appearances and grasp the deeper truths of existence. Humility involves recognizing one's place within the larger cosmic order, understanding that the quest for mastery is not about dominance or control but about aligning with the natural flow of the universe. Patience is essential, as the process of self-realization unfolds gradually, requiring persistence and dedication over time. Love, both for oneself and for others, is seen as the highest expression of personal mastery, as it reflects the interconnectedness of all beings and the realization that the self is part of a larger, universal whole.

The journey toward personal mastery also involves the discipline of the will, where the individual must learn to direct their energy and focus toward their higher purpose. The Rosicrucians teach that the will is a powerful force that can be used to shape one's reality, but it must be aligned with the principles of truth and goodness. Mastering the will involves learning to overcome the lower desires and impulses that arise from the ego, replacing them with the conscious intention to act in alignment with the divine will. This requires the cultivation of self-control, where the individual learns to resist temptation, distraction, and emotional reactions, maintaining a state of inner calm and clarity.

As the seeker progresses on the path to personal mastery, they begin to experience a deeper connection with their higher self, the divine spark within that represents their true essence. This connection allows the individual to access higher levels of consciousness, where they can receive guidance and inspiration from the inner planes. The Rosicrucians believe that the higher self is the source of wisdom and truth, and by aligning with this inner guidance, the individual gains insight into their life purpose and the greater meaning of existence. This alignment with the higher self is a key aspect of personal mastery, as it enables the individual to live in harmony with the divine laws that govern the universe.

The quest for self-realization is also closely tied to the concept of service, where the individual recognizes that their personal growth is not an end in itself but a means of contributing to the greater good. The Rosicrucians emphasize that true mastery involves using one's talents, knowledge, and wisdom to benefit others and to uplift humanity as a whole. This idea of service is rooted in the understanding that all beings are interconnected, and that by helping others to grow and evolve, the individual also advances their own spiritual development. Personal mastery, therefore, is not a solitary pursuit but a process that takes place within the context of the broader human community and the universal order.

In the Rosicrucian path, personal mastery is not about perfection in the conventional sense but about ongoing growth and evolution. The individual recognizes that the journey toward self-realization is never truly complete, as there are always deeper levels of understanding and higher states of consciousness to attain. The process of mastery is dynamic and continuous, where each new level of insight opens the door to further growth. This ongoing pursuit of mastery reflects the Rosicrucian belief in the infinite potential of the soul, where the individual is always evolving toward greater unity with the divine.

Central to personal mastery is the idea of balance— balancing the mind, body, and spirit, as well as the inner and outer aspects of life. The Rosicrucians teach that true mastery involves the harmonious integration of these different dimensions of existence. The individual must learn to navigate the material world with wisdom and integrity while maintaining a deep connection to the spiritual realm. This balance is reflected in the Rosicrucian emphasis on the importance of health and well-being, where the physical body is seen as a sacred vessel for the soul's journey. By caring for the body, nurturing the mind, and cultivating the spirit, the individual creates the conditions for personal mastery to flourish.

The quest for personal mastery in Rosicrucian thought is ultimately about realizing one's highest potential and aligning with the divine purpose that governs all life. It is a process of self-transformation that requires dedication, discipline, and a deep commitment to the principles of truth, love, and service. Through this journey, the individual not only attains greater wisdom and insight but also becomes a force for positive change in the world, contributing to the evolution of humanity and the unfolding of the divine plan.

Chapter 10: The Rosicrucian Legacy: Philosophy in Modern Spiritual Practice

The Rosicrucian legacy, deeply rooted in a synthesis of mysticism, science, and esoteric wisdom, continues to influence modern spiritual practice by offering a framework for inner transformation, personal mastery, and the pursuit of higher knowledge. This legacy, born from the early 17th-century Rosicrucian manifestos, has left a lasting imprint on Western esotericism, shaping the way individuals approach spirituality, self-realization, and the integration of spiritual and material worlds. The Rosicrucian philosophy emphasizes the interconnectedness of all things, the quest for hidden knowledge, and the belief that spiritual enlightenment can be attained through a combination of study, contemplation, and direct mystical experience. These principles continue to resonate in contemporary spiritual movements, particularly those that seek to balance personal growth with an understanding of universal truths.

At the heart of the Rosicrucian legacy is the idea that true wisdom is not confined to intellectual knowledge but must also encompass the mystical and experiential dimensions of life. In modern spiritual practice, this holistic approach is reflected in the growing emphasis on personal transformation, where individuals are encouraged to embark on an inner journey toward self-discovery and enlightenment. The Rosicrucian focus on the "invisible college," a hidden brotherhood of enlightened individuals working for the upliftment of humanity, has also evolved into a more inclusive idea in modern spirituality: that each person can become a bearer of wisdom and light through their own spiritual development. This sense of personal responsibility for one's own spiritual growth aligns with the broader modern emphasis on self-realization and the pursuit of knowledge beyond traditional religious structures.

One of the key aspects of the Rosicrucian philosophy that has carried over into modern spiritual practice is the integration of science and spirituality. The Rosicrucians believed that the study of the natural world and the pursuit of spiritual truth were not separate endeavors but two sides of the same coin. They saw the laws of nature as manifestations of divine order, and through the study of alchemy, astronomy, and other sciences, they sought to uncover the hidden patterns of the cosmos. In today's spiritual landscape, this integration of science and spirituality is reflected in movements that emphasize the importance of understanding the universe through both scientific inquiry and spiritual insight. Practices such as meditation, energy healing, and holistic health often draw upon this Rosicrucian belief that the material and spiritual worlds are interconnected, and that the principles governing one are reflected in the other.

The Rosicrucian emphasis on personal transformation through alchemy also plays a significant role in modern spiritual practice. Alchemy, in the Rosicrucian tradition, was not limited to the literal transmutation of metals but symbolized the inner process of transforming the soul from a base, unenlightened state to one of spiritual gold. This concept of inner alchemy, where the individual undergoes a series of purifications and transformations to align with higher consciousness, is echoed in many contemporary spiritual teachings. In modern practices such as yoga, mindfulness, and other forms of self-cultivation, there is a clear parallel to the Rosicrucian belief that personal growth requires discipline, reflection, and the purification of the ego. The stages of alchemical transformation—*nigredo* (blackening), *albedo* (whitening), *citrinitas* (yellowing), and *rubedo* (reddening)—continue to serve as metaphors for the spiritual journey, where the seeker must confront and overcome the lower aspects of the self to achieve a higher state of being.

The Rosicrucian legacy has also shaped the modern understanding of the relationship between the individual and the cosmos. Central to Rosicrucian thought is the Hermetic principle of "As above, so below," which suggests that the macrocosm of the universe is reflected in the microcosm of the individual. This idea that the same forces and patterns governing the cosmos also operate within the human soul has inspired a number of modern spiritual practices that focus on the idea of alignment with the universe. Astrology, for example, continues to draw upon the Rosicrucian belief in the influence of celestial bodies on human life, while practices such as energy work and sacred geometry are based on the idea that understanding and working with the patterns of the universe can lead to greater harmony and spiritual growth.

Another enduring aspect of the Rosicrucian legacy is the emphasis on service and the idea that personal enlightenment must be used for the benefit of others. The Rosicrucians believed that their knowledge and wisdom were not meant for personal gain but for the upliftment of humanity as a whole. This sense of responsibility for contributing to the greater good is reflected in many modern spiritual practices, where there is a strong focus on social responsibility, environmental stewardship, and the cultivation of compassion and empathy for others. In movements such as New Thought, Theosophy, and other spiritual philosophies that emphasize the power of the mind and the importance of living in harmony with the universe, there is a clear echo of the Rosicrucian belief that personal enlightenment carries with it an obligation to help others and to contribute to the betterment of society.

The Rosicrucian legacy has also influenced the modern understanding of ritual and symbolism in spiritual practice. The Rosicrucians were known for their use of symbols, such as the rose and the cross, to convey deeper spiritual truths, and this use of symbolism continues to play an important role in contemporary spiritual practices. Symbols, rituals, and ceremonies are often used as tools for focusing the mind and connecting with the divine, reflecting the Rosicrucian belief that ritual serves as a bridge between the material and spiritual realms. In many modern spiritual traditions, symbols such as the lotus flower, the mandala, and the sacred circle are used in much the same way as the Rosicrucians used the rose and the cross—to represent the soul's journey toward enlightenment and the harmonious integration of the spiritual and material aspects of existence.

The Rosicrucian legacy continues to shape modern spiritual thought through its emphasis on personal transformation, the integration of science and spirituality, and the belief in the interconnectedness of all things. This philosophy encourages individuals to seek wisdom not only through study and contemplation but through direct experience and inner transformation. By focusing on self-realization and contributing to the greater good, the Rosicrucian approach to spirituality remains relevant, providing a framework for those who seek to explore the deeper mysteries of existence while living a life of purpose, service, and alignment with universal principles.

BOOK 4
ROSICRUCIANISM AND ITS INFLUENCE ON MODERN
OCCULTISM
SAMUEL SHEPHERD

Chapter 1: The Rosicrucian Revival: The Rise of Modern Esotericism

The Rosicrucian revival in the late 19th and early 20th centuries marked a significant turning point in the development of modern esotericism. This resurgence was driven by a growing interest in mystical traditions, secret knowledge, and the synthesis of spiritual and scientific ideas. The roots of this revival can be traced to the original Rosicrucian manifestos of the early 17th century, which presented a vision of a secret brotherhood dedicated to the pursuit of divine wisdom, the reformation of society, and the uncovering of hidden truths about the universe. However, during the revival, these ancient ideals were reinterpreted and adapted to the intellectual and spiritual needs of a new era, one that was increasingly disillusioned with both the materialism of the Industrial Revolution and the rigid dogmas of institutionalized religion.

The Rosicrucian revival was closely linked to the broader esoteric movement that emerged during this period, which included the rise of Theosophy, the Hermetic Order of the Golden Dawn, and various other mystical and occult societies. These movements were inspired by the ideals of the original Rosicrucian brotherhood, but they also drew upon a wide range of mystical, alchemical, and magical traditions, blending them into a new, eclectic form of spirituality. The revivalists sought to recover the lost wisdom of the ancients, believing that the spiritual knowledge encoded in the teachings of the Rosicrucians, alchemists, and Hermeticists held the key to both personal enlightenment and the transformation of society.

One of the most significant figures in the Rosicrucian revival was Rudolf Steiner, who, through his founding of Anthroposophy, built upon many of the mystical and esoteric themes that were central to Rosicrucianism. Steiner emphasized the importance of spiritual science, which sought to bridge the gap between the material and spiritual worlds. In doing so, he reflected the Rosicrucian belief that true wisdom requires an integration of both scientific inquiry and spiritual insight. Steiner's teachings on the evolution of consciousness, reincarnation, and the hidden dimensions of reality were deeply influenced by the Rosicrucian tradition, and his work became a cornerstone for many modern esoteric schools of thought.

Another key influence on the Rosicrucian revival was the Hermetic Order of the Golden Dawn, an occult society founded in the late 19th century that sought to integrate various strands of Western esotericism, including Kabbalah, astrology, tarot, and alchemy. The Golden Dawn drew heavily on Rosicrucian symbolism and teachings, and many of its members considered themselves to be part of the broader Rosicrucian tradition. The Order's rituals and teachings emphasized the same themes of inner transformation, the pursuit of hidden knowledge, and the integration of spiritual and material realities that were central to the original Rosicrucian manifestos. The Golden Dawn's focus on personal initiation and the development of magical abilities also echoed the Rosicrucian emphasis on personal mastery and the cultivation of spiritual wisdom through direct experience.

The Theosophical Society, founded by Helena Petrovna Blavatsky in the late 19th century, also played a significant role in the Rosicrucian revival and the broader rise of modern esotericism. Blavatsky's teachings, which drew on Eastern philosophies, Western esotericism, and Rosicrucian ideals, emphasized the idea that humanity was on the cusp of a new spiritual evolution. The Theosophical Society sought to promote a synthesis of science, religion, and philosophy, reflecting the Rosicrucian belief in the unity of all knowledge. Blavatsky's emphasis on the existence of hidden masters—advanced spiritual beings who guide humanity from behind the scenes—paralleled the Rosicrucian notion of the invisible brotherhood, a secret group of enlightened individuals working for the betterment of society.

As the Rosicrucian revival gained momentum, it inspired the formation of new Rosicrucian organizations, each seeking to preserve and disseminate the teachings of the original brotherhood while adapting them to the modern world. One of the most prominent of these was the Ancient Mystical Order Rosae Crucis (AMORC), founded in the early 20th century by H. Spencer Lewis. AMORC sought to present the teachings of the Rosicrucians in a form that was accessible to the general public, offering a structured path of spiritual development that combined traditional Rosicrucian wisdom with modern scientific insights. AMORC emphasized the importance of inner transformation, the development of psychic abilities, and the pursuit of higher consciousness, while also promoting a vision of global peace and harmony through spiritual awakening.

The Rosicrucian revival also coincided with a broader cultural shift toward mysticism and alternative spirituality in the early 20th century. As industrialization, scientific rationalism, and materialism dominated the public consciousness, many people began to seek out alternative paths to meaning and fulfillment. The Rosicrucian teachings, with their emphasis on hidden knowledge, personal transformation, and the interconnectedness of all things, offered a compelling alternative to the purely materialistic worldview that had taken hold. The revival attracted not only mystics and occultists but also artists, writers, and intellectuals who were searching for deeper truths and new ways of understanding the world.

In the years following the revival, the influence of Rosicrucianism continued to grow, shaping the development of modern esoteric movements such as the New Age movement, which incorporated many of the key themes of the Rosicrucian tradition. The focus on personal transformation, the integration of science and spirituality, and the belief in the possibility of a global spiritual awakening remain central to many contemporary spiritual practices. The revival also left a lasting legacy in the arts, particularly in the works of writers, poets, and musicians who were inspired by the mystical ideals of the Rosicrucians and sought to express these themes through their creative work.

The Rosicrucian revival, while rooted in the esoteric traditions of the past, played a crucial role in shaping the spiritual landscape of the modern world. By reintroducing ancient wisdom into contemporary society, the revivalists helped to lay the foundation for the rise of modern esotericism, providing a new generation of seekers with the tools and teachings necessary for their own spiritual journey. The Rosicrucian legacy continues to inspire those who seek a deeper understanding of the mysteries of existence, offering a path of personal mastery, inner transformation, and the pursuit of hidden knowledge that resonates with the timeless quest for enlightenment.

Chapter 2: The Rosicrucian Impact on Freemasonry: A Shared Tradition

The relationship between Rosicrucianism and Freemasonry is one of profound influence, with both traditions sharing common ideals, symbolism, and philosophical underpinnings. While the origins of these two movements are distinct, the cross-pollination between Rosicrucian thought and Masonic ritual has had a lasting impact on the development of Freemasonry, particularly in its more esoteric branches. The Rosicrucian influence on Freemasonry can be traced back to the 17th century, when the publication of the Rosicrucian manifestos stirred widespread interest in mystical and alchemical philosophies across Europe. These manifestos, which spoke of a secret brotherhood dedicated to spiritual enlightenment, scientific advancement, and societal reform, resonated deeply with the emerging Masonic orders, which were themselves evolving from operative guilds into speculative, philosophically oriented societies.

One of the most significant points of convergence between Rosicrucianism and Freemasonry is the shared belief in the existence of hidden knowledge, or *gnosis*, that can only be accessed through initiation and personal transformation. Both traditions emphasize the importance of secrecy, not as a means of exclusion, but as a way to protect the sacred wisdom from being misunderstood or misused by those who are not spiritually prepared to receive it. In Rosicrucianism, this wisdom is associated with alchemical processes and mystical insights into the nature of the cosmos, while in Freemasonry, it is encoded in the symbolic rituals and teachings that are passed down through the various degrees of the Masonic system. This shared commitment to the preservation and transmission of hidden knowledge has fostered a deep connection between the two traditions, leading many Freemasons to explore Rosicrucian teachings as part of their own spiritual journey.

The Rosicrucian impact on Freemasonry is particularly evident in the development of the higher degrees of Freemasonry, especially those found in the Scottish Rite and the York Rite. The Scottish Rite, for example, includes degrees that are explicitly Rosicrucian in nature, such as the 18th degree, known as the Knight Rose Croix, which draws heavily on Rosicrucian symbolism and themes. In this degree, the candidate is introduced to the concepts of spiritual resurrection, inner transformation, and the quest for divine wisdom—all central tenets of Rosicrucian thought. The use of the rose and the cross in this degree mirrors the Rosicrucian emblem, which represents the union of the material and spiritual worlds, the crucifixion of the ego, and the blossoming of higher consciousness. This symbolic overlap reflects the deep influence that Rosicrucianism has had on the structure and content of Masonic ritual, particularly in the higher degrees, where the focus shifts from the moral and ethical lessons of the earlier degrees to more mystical and esoteric teachings.

Another area where the Rosicrucian influence on Freemasonry is evident is in the use of alchemical and Hermetic symbolism. Both traditions share a fascination with the process of inner alchemy, where the individual undergoes a series of transformations that lead to spiritual purification and enlightenment. In Freemasonry, this process is symbolized by the building of King Solomon's Temple, which represents both the physical and spiritual construction of the self. Just as the alchemist works to transmute base metals into gold, the Freemason is tasked with refining their character, transforming their lower, material nature into a higher, spiritual one. The tools of the Masonic craft—such as the square, compass, and trowel—are symbolic of this inner work, reflecting the Rosicrucian idea that spiritual progress requires both discipline and the application of sacred principles.

The Rosicrucian emphasis on the interconnectedness of all knowledge, particularly the unity of science, religion, and philosophy, has also influenced Freemasonry's intellectual framework. Freemasonry, like Rosicrucianism, seeks to bridge the gap between different fields of study, encouraging its members to explore a wide range of disciplines in their quest for truth. The Rosicrucian belief that the natural world is a reflection of divine wisdom, and that by studying nature, one can gain insight into spiritual truths, is mirrored in Masonic teachings. Freemasonry's emphasis on reason, inquiry, and the pursuit of knowledge aligns with the Rosicrucian vision of a universal brotherhood dedicated to the advancement of humanity through the integration of spiritual and scientific understanding.

The idea of a hidden or invisible brotherhood, which is central to Rosicrucianism, has also had a profound impact on the way Freemasonry understands itself as an initiatory tradition. The Rosicrucian manifestos spoke of a secret society of enlightened individuals working behind the scenes to guide the evolution of humanity, a concept that resonated with Masonic ideals of fraternity and service. This idea of an invisible college of wise men who possess esoteric knowledge has inspired many Freemasons to view their order as part of a larger, global network of spiritually awakened individuals who are committed to the betterment of society. The Rosicrucian emphasis on secrecy, initiation, and the gradual revelation of hidden truths through personal experience has been adopted by Freemasonry, particularly in its higher degrees, where the candidate is led through a series of symbolic trials that mirror the Rosicrucian process of spiritual awakening.

The Rosicrucian influence on Freemasonry is also reflected in the shared belief in the possibility of human perfection. Both traditions teach that the individual is capable of ascending to higher levels of consciousness and that this process of self-perfection is a lifelong journey. In Rosicrucianism, this journey is often described in alchemical terms, where the soul undergoes a series of purifications and transformations, leading to the creation of the Philosopher's Stone—a symbol of spiritual enlightenment and immortality. In Freemasonry, the concept of human perfection is expressed through the metaphor of the rough ashlar (an unshaped stone) being transformed into the perfect ashlar (a finely polished stone), symbolizing the refinement of the individual through the practice of virtue, self-discipline, and the application of Masonic principles.

The Rosicrucian impact on Freemasonry is undeniable, shaping its rituals, symbolism, and philosophical outlook. Both traditions share a common vision of personal transformation, the pursuit of hidden knowledge, and the belief in the interconnectedness of all things. Through the cross-fertilization of Rosicrucian and Masonic ideas, these two traditions have continued to inspire generations of seekers to embark on a path of self-discovery, inner alchemy, and the quest for spiritual enlightenment.

Chapter 3: The Hermetic Order of the Golden Dawn: A Rosicrucian Legacy

The Hermetic Order of the Golden Dawn, established in the late 19th century, stands as one of the most significant manifestations of the Rosicrucian legacy in modern esotericism. Drawing deeply from Rosicrucian principles, the Golden Dawn developed a system of magical and spiritual practice that emphasized the integration of mysticism, ritual, and personal transformation. The founders of the Golden Dawn were heavily influenced by the symbolic and philosophical teachings of the Rosicrucian tradition, particularly its emphasis on inner alchemy, the pursuit of hidden knowledge, and the belief in the possibility of spiritual enlightenment through initiation and disciplined practice. The Order sought to carry forward the Rosicrucian ideals of self-mastery, intellectual synthesis, and the exploration of the mysteries of existence, blending them with a wide range of occult traditions to create a unique and influential esoteric system.

At the heart of the Golden Dawn's teachings is the Rosicrucian concept of initiation, which represents both a symbolic death and rebirth—a journey of transformation in which the candidate passes through various degrees of understanding, purification, and enlightenment. The Golden Dawn's rituals were structured to guide initiates through this process of inner alchemy, using symbolic elements drawn from

Rosicrucianism, such as the rose and the cross, to represent the merging of the spiritual and material worlds. This process of initiation mirrors the Rosicrucian belief that true wisdom can only be attained through personal experience, self-transformation, and direct contact with the higher realms of consciousness. The stages of the Golden Dawn's initiatory system were designed to lead the aspirant step by step through a series of spiritual realizations, culminating in the integration of the higher self and the mastery of the forces of both the inner and outer worlds.

One of the key ways in which the Golden Dawn embodied the Rosicrucian legacy was through its emphasis on the synthesis of different esoteric traditions. Just as the Rosicrucians sought to unite science, religion, and philosophy in their quest for truth, the Golden Dawn drew on a wide range of sources, including Kabbalah, astrology, alchemy, and Hermeticism. This eclectic approach reflected the Rosicrucian ideal of a universal brotherhood of knowledge, where all paths to wisdom are valued and integrated into a cohesive spiritual system. The Golden Dawn's rituals and teachings incorporated elements from various mystical traditions, seeking to provide a comprehensive framework for the exploration of the divine mysteries. This emphasis on intellectual and spiritual synthesis is a hallmark of both Rosicrucianism and the Golden Dawn, reflecting a shared belief in the unity of all knowledge and the interconnectedness of the material and spiritual realms.

The influence of Rosicrucianism on the Golden Dawn is also evident in its use of symbolism, particularly the central symbol of the rose and the cross. The rose, representing spiritual enlightenment and the blossoming of divine knowledge, is combined with the cross, symbolizing the material world and the trials of earthly existence. This union of the rose and the cross in the Golden Dawn's rituals and teachings reflects the Rosicrucian belief in the necessity of balancing the spiritual and material aspects of life, achieving mastery over both in the quest for higher consciousness. The rose and cross also serve as powerful symbols of personal transformation, illustrating the alchemical process of turning base elements (the lower self) into gold (the purified, enlightened self). In this way, the Golden Dawn continued the Rosicrucian tradition of using alchemical and mystical symbols to represent the inner journey of spiritual awakening.

The Golden Dawn's teachings on magic and ritual practice were heavily influenced by Rosicrucian ideas of self-perfection and the ability to harness spiritual forces for personal and collective transformation. Like the Rosicrucians, members of the Golden Dawn believed that the universe is governed by hidden laws, which can be understood and manipulated through the proper application of magical and spiritual techniques. The rituals of the Golden Dawn were designed to teach initiates how to align themselves with these cosmic forces, using the symbols and tools of ceremonial magic to bring about changes in both the inner and outer worlds. This approach to magic reflects the Rosicrucian belief in the power of the mind and spirit to shape reality, as well as the importance of discipline and mastery in the pursuit of spiritual growth.

Another significant aspect of the Golden Dawn's connection to the Rosicrucian legacy is its focus on personal enlightenment and the development of the higher self. Both the Rosicrucians and the Golden Dawn viewed spiritual growth as a process of becoming more attuned to the divine aspects of the self, moving beyond the limitations of the ego and the material world to achieve a state of union with the higher realms. The Golden Dawn's teachings on the higher self, which is seen as the source of wisdom and guidance for the initiate, are closely aligned with the Rosicrucian belief in the divine spark that resides within each individual. Through rituals, meditation, and the disciplined practice of magic, the Golden Dawn sought to help its members develop a direct connection with this higher aspect of their being, leading them toward greater spiritual understanding and the realization of their full potential.

The Rosicrucian influence on the Golden Dawn is also evident in its organizational structure and its emphasis on secrecy and initiation. Like the Rosicrucians, the Golden Dawn operated as a secret society, with membership restricted to those who had demonstrated a commitment to the study of esoteric knowledge and personal transformation. The use of initiatory rites, degrees, and oaths of secrecy reflects the Rosicrucian tradition of maintaining the sacred mysteries for those who are spiritually prepared to receive them. The hierarchical structure of the Golden Dawn, with its system of grades that correspond to different levels of spiritual attainment, mirrors the Rosicrucian emphasis on the progressive nature of spiritual enlightenment, where each stage of the journey reveals new layers of wisdom and insight.

The Hermetic Order of the Golden Dawn, while drawing on a wide range of occult and mystical traditions, was deeply influenced by the Rosicrucian philosophy of inner transformation, initiation, and the pursuit of hidden knowledge. The Golden Dawn continued the Rosicrucian legacy by creating a system that blended magic, mysticism, and personal development, offering a structured path toward spiritual mastery and the realization of the higher self. Through its rituals, symbols, and teachings, the Golden Dawn played a pivotal role in reviving and expanding the Rosicrucian ideals in modern esotericism, ensuring that these ancient principles continued to inspire seekers on their quest for enlightenment.

Chapter 4: Rosicrucianism in Theosophy: The Search for Hidden Knowledge

Rosicrucianism played a significant role in shaping the foundation of Theosophy, especially in its emphasis on the search for hidden knowledge and the exploration of the spiritual dimensions of existence. Theosophy, founded by Helena Petrovna Blavatsky in the late 19th century, integrated various esoteric traditions from both the East and the West, but Rosicrucianism, with its emphasis on secrecy, spiritual initiation, and the pursuit of divine wisdom, had a profound impact on the structure and philosophy of the Theosophical movement. Blavatsky's writings reflect many of the core principles found in Rosicrucian thought, particularly the belief in an underlying unity of all religious and mystical traditions, the idea that spiritual truth is accessible to those willing to undergo personal transformation, and the notion that hidden, esoteric knowledge can lead to enlightenment.

One of the central tenets of both Rosicrucianism and Theosophy is the idea that true wisdom is hidden from the masses and can only be accessed through initiation and spiritual practice. This notion of hidden knowledge, or *gnosis*, is central to the Rosicrucian worldview, where the seeker must undergo a process of purification and enlightenment to access the deeper mysteries of the universe. In Theosophy, this idea is reflected in the teachings about the existence of the

"Masters of the Ancient Wisdom," advanced spiritual beings who are believed to hold the secrets of the universe and guide humanity's spiritual evolution from behind the scenes. Blavatsky's emphasis on the existence of these hidden masters parallels the Rosicrucian belief in an invisible brotherhood, a group of enlightened individuals working to elevate human consciousness and reform society.

The Rosicrucian influence on Theosophy is also evident in the focus on spiritual evolution and the development of higher consciousness. Both traditions emphasize the idea that the soul undergoes a process of transformation over many lifetimes, gradually ascending to higher levels of awareness and spiritual purity. In Rosicrucianism, this process is often described using the language of alchemy, where the soul is symbolically transmuted from base metal into gold through a series of purifications and initiations. Theosophy adopts a similar framework, teaching that the soul evolves through a series of incarnations, each lifetime offering the opportunity for spiritual growth and the refinement of consciousness. This process of evolution is governed by the law of karma and the cycle of reincarnation, concepts that are central to Theosophical philosophy and resonate with the Rosicrucian emphasis on the cyclical nature of spiritual transformation.

The search for hidden knowledge in both Rosicrucianism and Theosophy is also linked to the idea of esoteric wisdom being encoded in the natural world.

Rosicrucians believed that the physical world is a reflection of divine order, and that by studying nature, one can uncover the spiritual laws that govern the universe. This belief is closely aligned with Theosophy's teaching that the universe is an expression of divine intelligence, and that the patterns and rhythms of nature are manifestations of cosmic principles. Blavatsky's writings, particularly in *The Secret Doctrine*, emphasize that the hidden knowledge of the universe is written in the stars, the elements, and the cycles of nature, and that by attuning oneself to these patterns, one can gain access to the deeper truths of existence. This notion of studying the natural world to uncover spiritual wisdom is a hallmark of both traditions, reflecting their shared belief in the interconnectedness of all things.

Another significant point of intersection between Rosicrucianism and Theosophy is the use of symbolism and allegory to convey spiritual truths. In Rosicrucianism, symbols such as the rose and the cross, the Philosopher's Stone, and the stages of alchemical transformation are used to represent the soul's journey toward enlightenment. These symbols are not meant to be understood literally but are intended to point the seeker toward deeper, hidden meanings that can only be grasped through inner contemplation and mystical experience. Similarly, Theosophy employs a rich symbolic language to describe the stages of spiritual evolution and the structure of the universe. Theosophical teachings often use allegorical narratives, such as the story of the "root races" and the descent of spirit into matter, to illustrate the soul's journey through time and space. This reliance on symbolism reflects the influence of Rosicrucian thought, where spiritual truths are considered too profound to be communicated directly and must be encoded in symbolic form to protect them from being misunderstood or misused.

The Rosicrucian focus on initiation and personal transformation also had a significant impact on Theosophical practice, particularly in the establishment of structured paths for spiritual development. Rosicrucianism emphasizes that spiritual knowledge is not something that can be passively received but must be earned through disciplined practice, self-purification, and initiation into progressively higher levels of understanding. In Theosophy, this principle is reflected in the emphasis on individual responsibility for spiritual growth and the idea that each person must undergo their own process of initiation to access the deeper layers of wisdom. Blavatsky's teachings on meditation, self-discipline, and the cultivation of virtues such as compassion and detachment are in line with the Rosicrucian belief that the seeker must actively engage in their own spiritual transformation to gain access to hidden knowledge.

Theosophy's commitment to the synthesis of different religious and philosophical traditions also echoes the Rosicrucian ideal of a universal brotherhood of knowledge. The Rosicrucians believed that all spiritual traditions contain elements of the same underlying truth, and that by studying and synthesizing these traditions, one could gain a more complete understanding of the divine. This belief in the unity of all wisdom is a core principle of Theosophy, which seeks to integrate Eastern and Western spiritual traditions, as well as ancient and modern philosophies, into a single, cohesive system of knowledge. Blavatsky's teachings on the "perennial wisdom" or "ancient wisdom" reflect this Rosicrucian ideal of uncovering the universal truths that lie at the heart of all spiritual traditions.

The Rosicrucian influence on Theosophy, particularly in its emphasis on hidden knowledge, initiation, and the synthesis of spiritual traditions, helped shape the way Theosophy approached the pursuit of wisdom and spiritual enlightenment. Both traditions share a common vision of the universe as a place where divine truths are encoded in both the inner and outer worlds, waiting to be discovered by those willing to undergo the necessary personal transformation. Theosophy, in carrying forward these Rosicrucian ideals, contributed to the development of modern esoteric thought, creating a pathway for individuals seeking to uncover the hidden dimensions of reality and connect with the deeper mysteries of existence.

Chapter 5: Aleister Crowley and the Rosicrucian Influence in Thelema

Aleister Crowley, one of the most influential occult figures of the 20th century, was deeply influenced by Rosicrucian thought, which played a foundational role in shaping his religious and philosophical system known as Thelema. Crowley's engagement with Rosicrucianism began during his time as a member of the Hermetic Order of the Golden Dawn, an organization that drew heavily on Rosicrucian teachings. The Golden Dawn was a Rosicrucian-inspired magical order that focused on ceremonial magic, alchemy, Kabbalah, and inner alchemical transformation. These themes profoundly impacted Crowley's later development of Thelema, where the Rosicrucian influence can be seen in the system's symbolic structure, its emphasis on initiation, and the synthesis of mysticism, esotericism, and personal spiritual mastery.

Central to Thelema is the concept of the True Will, the idea that each individual has a unique, divine purpose that must be discovered and lived in harmony with the universe. This idea reflects the Rosicrucian emphasis on personal transformation and enlightenment, where the individual undergoes a series of spiritual trials to uncover their divine essence. The Rosicrucians viewed the path to enlightenment as a journey of inner alchemy, where the ego is gradually purified and the true self, aligned with the divine, is revealed. In

Thelema, Crowley similarly emphasized the importance of finding and following one's True Will as the key to spiritual fulfillment and cosmic alignment. The True Will can be seen as a modern interpretation of the Rosicrucian quest for inner alchemical transformation, where the individual must transcend the limitations of the lower self and become an embodiment of their divine purpose.

The structure of Thelema's initiatory system also draws upon Rosicrucian principles, particularly the idea that spiritual knowledge is revealed progressively through a series of rites and degrees. Crowley, like the Rosicrucians, believed that true wisdom could not be attained instantly but required the seeker to undergo a gradual process of purification and enlightenment. Thelema's initiatory rituals, many of which are based on the practices of the Golden Dawn, reflect this belief, guiding the initiate through stages of self-discovery, inner awakening, and mastery of the spiritual forces of the universe. In Thelema, as in Rosicrucianism, initiation is seen not only as a symbolic act but as a transformative experience that brings the individual into direct contact with higher spiritual realities.

The Rosicrucian emphasis on symbolism and allegory as vehicles for conveying esoteric truths also found a strong resonance in Crowley's Thelemic teachings. Crowley, like the Rosicrucians, believed that certain symbols held the key to unlocking hidden dimensions of reality, allowing the seeker to gain access to deeper spiritual knowledge. The use of magical symbols, sacred geometry, and mythological archetypes in Thelema reflects the Rosicrucian belief in the power of symbols to connect the material and spiritual worlds. One of the most important symbols in Thelema is the rose-cross, which Crowley inherited from his Rosicrucian influences. In Thelema, the rose-cross represents the union of opposites—spirit and matter, masculine and feminine, life and death—which mirrors the Rosicrucian view of spiritual transformation as a process of reconciling dualities and achieving balance.

Crowley's magnum opus, *The Book of the Law* (*Liber AL vel Legis*), which serves as the central text of Thelema, also contains echoes of Rosicrucian ideas, particularly in its vision of spiritual evolution and the coming of a new Aeon. In *The Book of the Law*, Crowley proclaimed the dawn of the Aeon of Horus, an era characterized by the pursuit of individual sovereignty, self-realization, and spiritual liberation. This vision of a new era of spiritual awakening parallels the Rosicrucian ideals expressed in their 17th-century manifestos, which called for the reform of society and the renewal of human consciousness through the integration of science, mysticism, and divine wisdom. Both Crowley and the Rosicrucians envisioned a world where humanity would be guided by spiritual enlightenment, where hidden knowledge would become accessible to those prepared to receive it, and where individuals would play an active role in shaping their spiritual and material destinies.

The Thelemic concept of magical practice, which is integral to Crowley's system, also bears the imprint of Rosicrucianism. Crowley emphasized the importance of ceremonial magic as a tool for personal transformation and the realization of the True Will. In this sense, magic was not merely about manipulating external forces but about aligning the individual with the divine principles of the universe. This approach to magic mirrors the Rosicrucian belief in alchemical transformation, where the practitioner uses ritual and symbolism to refine their inner being and bring themselves into harmony with cosmic laws. Crowley's rituals, such as the Gnostic Mass and the rites of initiation in the Ordo Templi Orientis (O.T.O.), are filled with Rosicrucian-inspired symbols, gestures, and invocations that reflect this shared emphasis on inner alchemy and the pursuit of hidden knowledge.

Crowley's deep interest in Kabbalah, another significant aspect of both Rosicrucianism and Thelema, further underscores the Rosicrucian influence on his work. The Kabbalistic Tree of Life, which plays a central role in both systems, serves as a map of the universe and the individual's journey toward spiritual enlightenment. In Thelema, the Tree of Life is used as a framework for understanding the stages of initiation, the structure of the soul, and the forces at work in both the macrocosm and the microcosm. Crowley's use of the Tree of Life reflects the Rosicrucian tradition of employing Kabbalistic symbolism to describe the process of spiritual ascent, where the seeker must navigate the various spheres or *sephiroth* to reach union with the divine. In addition to these shared philosophical elements, Crowley's focus on personal mastery and the cultivation of the higher self in Thelema is closely aligned with Rosicrucian ideals. Both Crowley and the Rosicrucians emphasized the importance of self-discipline, self-knowledge, and the continual refinement of the self as the path to spiritual enlightenment. Crowley's magical motto, "Do what thou wilt shall be the whole of the Law," encapsulates this idea, suggesting that true freedom and fulfillment come from discovering and following one's True Will. This pursuit of self-realization, combined with the use of ritual, symbolism, and esoteric knowledge, forms the core of both Rosicrucianism and Thelema, demonstrating the enduring influence of Rosicrucian thought on Crowley's system of spiritual philosophy.

Thelema, in many ways, represents a continuation of the Rosicrucian tradition, adapted for a modern audience and infused with Crowley's own unique vision of individual sovereignty, magical practice, and the pursuit of hidden wisdom. Through his work, Crowley carried forward the Rosicrucian legacy of spiritual transformation, initiation, and the quest for personal enlightenment, offering a system that continues to inspire seekers on the path to discovering their True Will and realizing their full potential.

Chapter 6: Rosicrucianism in Modern Magic: Rituals and Practices

Rosicrucianism has had a profound influence on the development of modern magic, particularly in shaping the structure, rituals, and practices of various esoteric traditions that emerged in the late 19th and 20th centuries. Rooted in the 17th-century Rosicrucian manifestos, which combined elements of alchemy, mysticism, and Hermeticism, the Rosicrucian philosophy emphasized personal transformation, spiritual enlightenment, and the integration of science and magic. These core principles became foundational for many modern magical orders, such as the Hermetic Order of the Golden Dawn, the Ordo Templi Orientis (O.T.O.), and other magical societies that sought to merge ritualistic practices with spiritual development. Rosicrucianism's emphasis on initiation, the use of symbolism, and the pursuit of hidden knowledge continues to permeate the rituals and practices of contemporary magical traditions.

One of the most significant ways in which Rosicrucianism has influenced modern magic is through its system of initiation, which is designed to guide the practitioner through a series of spiritual transformations. In Rosicrucianism, initiation is seen as a symbolic journey of death and rebirth, where the initiate must confront the limitations of the ego, undergo purification, and align with higher spiritual principles. This process of inner alchemy is mirrored in the structure of modern magical orders, particularly the Hermetic Order of the Golden Dawn, where the initiate passes through various degrees, each representing a different stage of spiritual awakening and mastery. The use of initiation as a means of spiritual growth is central to both Rosicrucianism and modern magic, where the practitioner is progressively introduced to deeper layers of esoteric knowledge and occult power.

The rituals of modern magic are also heavily influenced by Rosicrucian symbolism, particularly the rose and cross, which represent the union of spirit and matter, the path of personal transformation, and the reconciliation of opposites. The rose-cross emblem, a central symbol in Rosicrucianism, is often invoked in magical rituals to symbolize the alchemical marriage of the divine and the earthly, as well as the seeker's journey toward enlightenment. In the Golden Dawn, for example, the rose-cross is used as a focal point in rituals designed to harmonize the practitioner's inner and outer worlds, reflecting the Rosicrucian belief in the need for balance between the material and spiritual dimensions of life. The rose-cross ritual often involves visualization techniques and the invocation of divine names, echoing the Rosicrucian practice of using sacred geometry and sacred sound to align with cosmic forces.

Another key element of Rosicrucianism that has been adopted into modern magical practices is the concept of the *inner temple*, an idea that reflects the belief in the individual's capacity to construct a personal sacred space within their own consciousness. In Rosicrucianism, the inner temple represents the perfected soul, the place where divine wisdom is accessed, and where the practitioner communes with higher spiritual forces. This concept has been integrated into modern magic through practices such as visualization and meditation, where the magician builds a symbolic inner sanctuary as a space for inner work, transformation, and spiritual communication. The construction of the inner temple is often accompanied by ritual gestures, chanting, and the invocation of spiritual entities, all designed to elevate the consciousness of the practitioner to higher states of awareness.

The use of alchemy as a symbolic and practical tool for spiritual development is another aspect of Rosicrucianism that has influenced modern magical rituals. While physical alchemy—focused on transforming base metals into gold—was an important aspect of early Rosicrucian practices, modern magic has adapted this process into a form of spiritual alchemy, where the focus is on transforming the self rather than material substances. In this context, the stages of alchemical transformation—*nigredo* (blackening), *albedo* (whitening), *citrinitas* (yellowing), and *rubedo* (reddening)—are used to symbolize the inner process of purification, illumination, and spiritual rebirth. Rituals that invoke these alchemical stages often involve symbolic actions, such as lighting candles, reciting incantations, or using colored objects that correspond to the phases of alchemy, allowing the practitioner to engage with the archetypal forces of transformation.

Rosicrucianism's integration of Kabbalistic teachings has also left a lasting mark on modern magic, particularly in the use of the Kabbalistic Tree of Life as a framework for understanding the universe and the self. The Tree of Life, which consists of ten spheres or *sephiroth*, is often used in magical rituals as a map of spiritual ascent, guiding the practitioner through the various levels of consciousness toward union with the divine. In Rosicrucianism, the Kabbalistic Tree of Life is seen as a symbolic representation of the path of initiation, with each sphere corresponding to a different stage of spiritual development. Modern magical orders, such as the Golden Dawn and the O.T.O., have adopted this framework, using it as a foundation for their ritual work, where the initiate's progress is tracked along the Tree of Life as they move through different degrees of initiation.

The emphasis on secrecy and the transmission of hidden knowledge is another key aspect of Rosicrucianism that has influenced modern magical practice. The Rosicrucians believed that esoteric wisdom should be guarded and transmitted only to those who were spiritually prepared to receive it, a principle that has carried over into modern magical orders. In many contemporary magical traditions, knowledge is revealed progressively through a series of initiations, each level unlocking new layers of understanding and deeper access to occult powers. This hierarchical approach to spiritual knowledge reflects the Rosicrucian emphasis on personal readiness and the belief that true wisdom can only be attained through disciplined practice and personal transformation.

The Rosicrucian approach to magic, which emphasizes the alignment of the practitioner with cosmic forces and divine principles, has also shaped the way modern magic views the role of the magician. In Rosicrucianism, magic is not simply a tool for manipulating the material world but a means of harmonizing the self with the divine order of the universe. Modern magical practices, influenced by this philosophy, often involve rituals designed to bring the practitioner into resonance with higher spiritual entities, such as angels, planetary spirits, or archetypal forces. These rituals, which may include invocations, consecrations, and the use of sacred symbols, are seen as a way of aligning the practitioner's will with the divine, reflecting the Rosicrucian ideal of using magic for spiritual upliftment rather than personal gain.

Chapter 7: The New Age Movement: Rosicrucian Ideals in Contemporary Spirituality

The New Age movement, which emerged in the latter half of the 20th century, draws heavily on Rosicrucian ideals, infusing contemporary spirituality with ancient esoteric wisdom and practices. Rosicrucianism's emphasis on personal transformation, the search for hidden knowledge, and the integration of science, mysticism, and religion deeply influenced the philosophy of the New Age. The movement's central tenets—such as spiritual evolution, the unity of all life, and the potential for individual enlightenment—reflect the Rosicrucian vision of humanity's capacity for growth and alignment with higher, divine forces. Many practices and beliefs commonly associated with the New Age, including meditation, energy healing, holistic health, and the use of sacred geometry, have roots in the teachings of Rosicrucianism, which sought to harmonize the material and spiritual worlds through personal development and the pursuit of wisdom.

One of the most significant Rosicrucian influences on the New Age movement is the belief in spiritual evolution, which posits that individuals and humanity as a whole are on a continuous journey of growth, moving toward greater awareness and higher states of consciousness. In Rosicrucianism, this idea is central to the philosophy of initiation, where the seeker undergoes a process of transformation and purification to align with the divine. The New Age movement adopted this concept, teaching that through personal effort, meditation, and spiritual practice, individuals can ascend to higher levels of consciousness, eventually achieving enlightenment. This journey of spiritual evolution is seen as a way to reconnect with the divine source, often referred to in New Age circles as the "Universal Mind" or "Cosmic Consciousness," echoing Rosicrucian teachings about the unity of the self with the larger, cosmic order.

The Rosicrucian ideal of hidden knowledge, or *gnosis*, is another aspect that has shaped the New Age movement's approach to spirituality. The belief that spiritual truths are not immediately apparent but must be uncovered through inner exploration and direct experience is a cornerstone of both Rosicrucianism and the New Age. Many New Age practices, such as channeling, intuitive healing, and past-life regression, are rooted in the idea that there are deeper layers of reality that can only be accessed by those who are spiritually attuned. This mirrors the Rosicrucian belief that esoteric wisdom is reserved for those who are prepared to receive it, often through a process of initiation or personal transformation. The New Age movement's focus on discovering one's spiritual potential and accessing hidden dimensions of reality reflects the Rosicrucian quest for inner alchemical transformation and enlightenment.

Another key Rosicrucian influence on the New Age movement is the emphasis on the interconnectedness of all life, a concept that is expressed in the New Age ideal of the oneness of humanity, nature, and the universe. Rosicrucians believed in the unity of all things, both material and spiritual, teaching that the microcosm (the individual) reflects the macrocosm (the universe) in a harmonious relationship. This Hermetic principle, encapsulated in the axiom "As above, so below," is central to Rosicrucian thought and has been widely embraced by the New Age movement. In contemporary spirituality, this idea manifests in the belief that every individual is part of a larger cosmic order and that by aligning oneself with this universal energy, one can achieve balance, peace, and spiritual growth. The New Age focus on harmony with nature, environmental consciousness, and the exploration of interconnected energy fields is a direct reflection of this Rosicrucian principle.

Holistic health and healing practices, which are a major component of the New Age movement, also have roots in Rosicrucian ideals. The Rosicrucians believed in the healing power of nature and the human body's innate ability to achieve balance when aligned with the spiritual laws of the universe. They saw health as a reflection of one's physical, mental, and spiritual alignment, teaching that disease often resulted from disharmony between the body and the soul. The New Age movement adopted this perspective, promoting practices such as energy healing, crystal therapy, and Reiki, all of which focus on restoring the natural flow of energy within the body to promote healing. This holistic approach to health, which integrates the body, mind, and spirit, mirrors the Rosicrucian belief in the interdependence of all aspects of existence and the importance of achieving balance and harmony on all levels.

Meditation, another cornerstone of New Age practice, reflects the Rosicrucian emphasis on inner stillness and contemplation as tools for spiritual growth. In Rosicrucianism, meditation is seen as a way to access higher states of consciousness, allowing the individual to connect with divine wisdom and gain insight into the hidden truths of existence. The New Age movement adopted this practice, promoting meditation as a means of self-discovery, stress relief, and spiritual enlightenment. Through meditation, New Age practitioners seek to quiet the mind, align with universal energies, and access deeper layers of consciousness, reflecting the Rosicrucian belief that inner silence is essential for receiving spiritual knowledge and achieving personal transformation.

Sacred geometry, which has become a popular symbol in New Age art and spiritual practices, also has its roots in Rosicrucian teachings. Rosicrucians believed that the universe is structured according to geometric principles, with shapes such as the circle, triangle, and pentagram representing divine harmony and the underlying order of creation. The New Age movement embraced sacred geometry as a way to connect with the spiritual dimensions of reality, using geometric symbols in meditation, healing practices, and ritual to tap into the universal patterns that govern the cosmos. The use of sacred geometry in New Age spirituality reflects the Rosicrucian belief that by understanding the geometric patterns of the universe, one can gain insight into the divine laws that shape existence and align oneself with the creative forces of the cosmos.

The integration of science and spirituality, a central feature of the New Age movement, also reflects the influence of Rosicrucianism. The Rosicrucians believed that science and mysticism were not mutually exclusive but complementary paths to understanding the divine order of the universe. They sought to integrate alchemical and scientific knowledge with spiritual insight, believing that by studying the natural world, one could uncover the deeper spiritual truths that governed reality. This synthesis of science and spirituality is evident in the New Age movement's embrace of concepts such as quantum physics, energy fields, and consciousness studies, all of which seek to bridge the gap between material and spiritual knowledge. New Age thinkers often refer to modern scientific discoveries as validation of ancient esoteric principles, reflecting the Rosicrucian belief that the material world is a reflection of spiritual reality and that both can be understood through a unified approach to knowledge.

In its pursuit of spiritual evolution, hidden wisdom, and the integration of diverse traditions, the New Age movement continues to carry forward many of the core ideals of Rosicrucianism. These Rosicrucian principles have been adapted to fit the needs and sensibilities of contemporary seekers, providing a framework for personal transformation and spiritual exploration that resonates with the modern world.

Chapter 8: Gnostic Revival: Rosicrucianism's Role in Modern Gnostic Thought

The revival of Gnostic thought in the modern era has been significantly shaped by the influence of Rosicrucianism, which played a crucial role in reintroducing many Gnostic ideas into the esoteric traditions of the West. Rosicrucianism, emerging in the 17th century through a series of enigmatic manifestos, was imbued with the philosophical and spiritual currents of Hermeticism, alchemy, and Gnosticism, integrating these ancient teachings into a new framework of mysticism, personal enlightenment, and the search for hidden knowledge. The Gnostic themes present in Rosicrucianism—particularly the emphasis on divine gnosis, or inner knowledge, the dualism between spirit and matter, and the journey of the soul toward illumination—have deeply influenced modern Gnostic movements, which seek to revive and reinterpret these ancient doctrines for contemporary spiritual seekers.

One of the most profound ways Rosicrucianism has impacted modern Gnostic thought is through its emphasis on the individual's direct experience of the divine. In both Gnosticism and Rosicrucianism, the soul's awakening to its true nature is seen as the primary goal of the spiritual path. The Gnostics taught that the material world was a realm of illusion, created by a lesser deity known as the Demiurge, and that the true essence of reality could only be understood through direct, inner experience of the divine spark that resides within the soul. Rosicrucianism, drawing on these same principles, emphasized that true knowledge is not acquired through external sources but through personal revelation and spiritual practice. This idea of direct, experiential knowledge, or gnosis, became a key component of the Rosicrucian initiatory process, where the individual undergoes a series of transformative experiences designed to bring them into contact with their inner divine essence. This focus on personal transformation and inner revelation, central to both traditions, has continued to resonate in modern Gnostic thought, where the pursuit of gnosis remains the ultimate spiritual goal.

The Rosicrucian belief in the existence of a hidden, esoteric tradition that has been passed down through the ages also reflects a distinctly Gnostic worldview. Gnosticism has always emphasized the idea that true spiritual knowledge is concealed from the masses and can only be accessed by those who have been initiated into its mysteries. Rosicrucianism adopted this same perspective, presenting itself as the inheritor of a secret wisdom tradition that had been preserved by an invisible brotherhood of enlightened adepts. This notion of a hidden spiritual lineage, extending back to ancient times, has been a central theme in the modern Gnostic revival, where there is a strong emphasis on uncovering the esoteric teachings that have been suppressed or lost over the centuries. Modern Gnostic groups, inspired by Rosicrucianism, often see themselves as part of this ancient lineage, dedicated to reviving and disseminating the hidden truths that can lead to spiritual liberation.

The dualistic worldview of Gnosticism, which posits a fundamental distinction between the material world and the spiritual realm, also finds expression in Rosicrucian teachings and has influenced the way modern Gnostics interpret the nature of existence. In Gnosticism, the material world is viewed as a flawed creation, a prison for the soul, which must be transcended through the attainment of gnosis. The Rosicrucians, while not as explicitly dualistic as the Gnostics, nonetheless shared a similar perspective, teaching that the material world is a reflection of a higher spiritual reality and that the individual must learn to navigate both the physical and spiritual dimensions of life. This dualistic understanding of the cosmos has been a key feature of modern Gnostic thought, where the emphasis on spiritual transcendence and the rejection of materialism continues to inform contemporary Gnostic practices and beliefs.

The Rosicrucian influence on modern Gnosticism can also be seen in the symbolic and allegorical language used to describe the journey of the soul. In both traditions, symbols and allegories are employed to convey spiritual truths that cannot be easily expressed through ordinary language. The Rosicrucian manifestos, for example, are filled with alchemical and Hermetic symbols that represent the process of spiritual transformation, where the soul must undergo a series of purifications and initiations before it can ascend to higher levels of consciousness. Similarly, Gnostic texts, such as the *Nag

Hammadi* scriptures, use symbolic language to describe the soul's journey from ignorance to enlightenment, often depicting the material world as a labyrinth or a veil that must be pierced to reach the divine realm. This shared use of symbolism and allegory has been carried forward into modern Gnostic thought, where practitioners continue to use these tools to deepen their understanding of spiritual realities and to guide their personal journey toward gnosis.

Another area in which Rosicrucianism has influenced modern Gnostic thought is in the emphasis on the role of the divine feminine. In Gnosticism, the figure of Sophia, the embodiment of divine wisdom, plays a central role in the creation of the cosmos and the salvation of humanity. Sophia's descent into the material world and her subsequent redemption mirror the journey of the soul, which must awaken to its divine origin and return to the spiritual realm. Rosicrucianism, while not explicitly Gnostic in its depiction of the divine feminine, nonetheless incorporates similar themes in its teachings on wisdom and enlightenment. The rose, a central symbol in Rosicrucianism, is often associated with divine wisdom and the unfolding of spiritual knowledge, echoing the Gnostic reverence for Sophia. This focus on the divine feminine has been a significant aspect of the modern Gnostic revival, where there is a renewed interest in the role of Sophia and other feminine archetypes in the process of spiritual awakening.

The integration of Kabbalistic teachings into Rosicrucianism has also contributed to the modern

Gnostic interpretation of the Tree of Life as a symbol of spiritual ascent. Both Gnosticism and Kabbalah emphasize the idea of the soul's journey through various levels of reality, moving from the material world to the higher, spiritual realms. The Rosicrucians adopted the Kabbalistic Tree of Life as a central symbol in their teachings, using it to represent the stages of spiritual development and the path to divine union. This Kabbalistic framework has been embraced by many modern Gnostic groups, who see the Tree of Life as a map of the soul's ascent from the physical world to the realm of divine light and knowledge. By integrating these Rosicrucian and Kabbalistic concepts, modern Gnosticism has developed a rich symbolic language that continues to guide seekers on their spiritual journey toward gnosis.

Rosicrucianism's influence on modern Gnosticism is evident in its emphasis on personal transformation, the pursuit of hidden knowledge, and the symbolic depiction of the soul's journey toward enlightenment. Through its integration of Gnostic themes and its preservation of ancient esoteric wisdom, Rosicrucianism has played a key role in the revival of Gnostic thought in the contemporary spiritual landscape, providing a framework for individuals seeking to reconnect with the divine and uncover the deeper mysteries of existence.

Chapter 9: Rosicrucianism in Popular Culture: Literature, Art, and Cinema

Rosicrucianism has had a subtle yet profound impact on popular culture, influencing literature, art, and cinema through its rich symbolism, esoteric philosophy, and mysterious aura. Its ideals of hidden knowledge, spiritual transformation, and the pursuit of enlightenment have captured the imaginations of artists, writers, and filmmakers, who have woven Rosicrucian themes into their work, often blending mysticism with creativity to explore the deeper mysteries of existence. From early literature to contemporary cinema, Rosicrucianism has left its mark by providing a symbolic and philosophical foundation that speaks to the timeless human quest for self-realization, wisdom, and transcendence.

In literature, Rosicrucianism's influence can be traced back to the Romantic period, where the ideals of spiritual transformation and hidden knowledge resonated with many poets and authors. One of the most significant examples is the work of German writer Johann Wolfgang von Goethe, whose epic drama *Faust* incorporates many elements of Rosicrucian and alchemical symbolism. In *Faust*, the titular character's quest for ultimate knowledge and transcendence through a pact with Mephistopheles reflects the alchemical journey of transformation and purification central to Rosicrucianism. The themes of duality, the pursuit of hidden truths, and the soul's battle between light and darkness are at the heart of both Rosicrucianism and *Faust*, offering a rich exploration of the soul's journey toward enlightenment.

Similarly, the novels of French writer Honoré de Balzac are filled with references to secret societies and mystical knowledge, drawing inspiration from Rosicrucian themes. In his novel *Séraphîta*, Balzac explores the idea of androgyny as a symbol of spiritual perfection, a concept that resonates with Rosicrucian teachings on the union of opposites, where the masculine and feminine principles are harmonized to achieve higher consciousness. This blending of esoteric philosophy with literary exploration continued into the 20th century, where writers such as Umberto Eco and Dan Brown brought Rosicrucian and occult symbolism to mainstream audiences. Brown's *The Da Vinci Code* is a prominent example, where secret societies, hidden symbols, and the quest for ancient knowledge play central roles, drawing on the mystique of the Rosicrucians and their legacy of esoteric wisdom.

In the world of art, Rosicrucianism has inspired numerous painters, sculptors, and architects who have sought to express spiritual truths through symbolism and form. The mystical ideas of the Rosicrucians, particularly their belief in the interconnectedness of all things and the presence of divine patterns in nature, resonated with many artists of the Symbolist movement in the late 19th century. Artists such as Jean Delville and

Fernand Khnopff created works that embodied the Rosicrucian ideals of spiritual ascent, the transcendence of the material world, and the unveiling of hidden realities. Delville's painting *The School of Plato*, for instance, echoes the Rosicrucian concept of a hidden brotherhood of enlightened beings who guide humanity from the shadows, while Khnopff's enigmatic portraits evoke the idea of inner mysteries that can only be revealed through personal transformation.

Rosicrucian architecture also plays a role in the symbolic exploration of spiritual truths. The design of buildings such as the Rosicrucian Egyptian Museum in San Jose, California, reflects the influence of sacred geometry, a concept central to Rosicrucian thought. Sacred geometry, which the Rosicrucians believed was the key to understanding the divine order of the universe, is reflected in the harmonious proportions and symbolic shapes used in the museum's architecture. This focus on geometry as a pathway to spiritual knowledge has also inspired artists working in the fields of abstract and visionary art, where geometric patterns are used to represent the structure of reality and the hidden forces that shape existence.

Cinema, too, has been influenced by Rosicrucianism, with filmmakers using its themes of secret knowledge, mystical transformation, and esoteric symbolism to explore complex narratives of personal and spiritual discovery. One of the most well-known examples is Stanley Kubrick's *Eyes Wide Shut*, a film that delves into the world of secret societies and hidden rituals. While not explicitly Rosicrucian, the film's exploration of mysterious, elite circles, ritualistic symbolism, and the protagonist's journey into the unknown reflects many of the core elements found in Rosicrucian thought. Kubrick's use of visual symbolism, such as the repeated imagery of masks and veils, echoes the Rosicrucian idea that spiritual truths are hidden and can only be uncovered through initiation and personal transformation.

Alejandro Jodorowsky's films, such as *The Holy Mountain* and *El Topo*, also bear the influence of Rosicrucian and alchemical symbolism. These films are rich with esoteric imagery, exploring themes of spiritual awakening, death, and rebirth in a manner reminiscent of Rosicrucian initiation rituals. In *The Holy Mountain*, for instance, the protagonist's journey through a surreal landscape filled with symbolic challenges and spiritual guides mirrors the Rosicrucian path of inner alchemy, where the individual must confront their own darkness and transcend the material world to achieve higher consciousness. Jodorowsky's work, with its emphasis on spiritual transformation through esoteric symbolism, reflects the Rosicrucian belief in the power of symbols and rituals to catalyze personal enlightenment.

In the genre of occult and esoteric cinema, the influence of Rosicrucianism is also evident in films such as *The Ninth Gate*, directed by Roman Polanski, which centers on the search for a mystical book that unlocks hidden knowledge and supernatural power. The film's narrative structure, where the protagonist gradually uncovers deeper layers of occult knowledge, mirrors the Rosicrucian emphasis on initiation and the progressive revelation of esoteric wisdom. This use of hidden symbols, secret societies, and the quest for ancient knowledge in cinema taps into the Rosicrucian tradition of mystery, where the path to spiritual enlightenment is revealed through a process of inner exploration and symbolic discovery.

Rosicrucianism's influence on popular culture, through literature, art, and cinema, continues to inspire artists and creators who are drawn to its themes of hidden knowledge, personal transformation, and the search for spiritual enlightenment. The rich symbolic language of Rosicrucianism, combined with its mystique as a secret tradition, provides fertile ground for exploring the deeper mysteries of existence and the transformative power of esoteric wisdom. Through these creative mediums, the ideals of Rosicrucianism have permeated contemporary culture, offering a vision of spirituality that transcends the material world and points toward the infinite possibilities of personal and cosmic evolution.

Chapter 10: The Future of Rosicrucianism: Evolution of a Timeless Tradition

The future of Rosicrucianism lies in its ability to continue evolving while maintaining its core principles of personal transformation, the pursuit of hidden knowledge, and the integration of spirituality with scientific inquiry. As a tradition that has adapted through the centuries, Rosicrucianism has demonstrated a remarkable capacity to resonate with different eras and cultural contexts, constantly reinterpreting its esoteric teachings to meet the changing needs of humanity. The next phase of Rosicrucianism's development will likely focus on expanding its influence in an increasingly interconnected and technologically advanced world, where the boundaries between science, mysticism, and spirituality are becoming ever more fluid.

One of the key areas in which Rosicrucianism may continue to evolve is through its relationship with modern science and technology. Since its inception, Rosicrucianism has emphasized the harmony between spiritual and scientific pursuits, encouraging its followers to study the natural world as a reflection of divine order. In the 21st century, this principle can be further developed as new frontiers in science, such as quantum physics, consciousness studies, and the exploration of artificial intelligence, provide fertile ground for the integration of Rosicrucian philosophy.

Quantum physics, with its emphasis on interconnectedness, uncertainty, and the hidden dimensions of reality, resonates deeply with Rosicrucian ideas about the underlying spiritual principles that govern the universe. As scientific discoveries continue to unveil new layers of existence, Rosicrucianism may offer a framework for interpreting these developments through a spiritual lens, providing insights into the nature of reality and the role of consciousness in shaping the material world.

The concept of transhumanism, which explores the possibility of enhancing human capacities through technology, may also intersect with Rosicrucian teachings about the potential for human evolution. While Rosicrucianism emphasizes the spiritual development of the individual, the advent of technologies that extend life, enhance cognitive abilities, and alter the human body raises questions about the role of technology in the process of enlightenment. Rosicrucian teachings about the union of spirit and matter could offer a balanced perspective on these advancements, suggesting that true evolution requires not only physical enhancement but also the cultivation of spiritual virtues and inner wisdom. As humanity grapples with the implications of technological advancements, Rosicrucianism may serve as a guiding philosophy, encouraging the integration of technological progress with ethical and spiritual considerations.

Another potential area for the future evolution of Rosicrucianism is its engagement with global spirituality. In an increasingly globalized world, where the boundaries between cultures and spiritual traditions are dissolving, Rosicrucianism may continue to expand by incorporating elements from other mystical traditions while preserving its distinct Hermetic and alchemical foundations. Rosicrucianism has long been influenced by a wide range of esoteric traditions, including Kabbalah, Gnosticism, and alchemy, and this openness to synthesis has allowed the tradition to remain relevant across different time periods. In the future, Rosicrucianism may continue to draw inspiration from Eastern philosophies such as Buddhism, Taoism, and Hinduism, integrating their insights into the nature of consciousness, meditation, and enlightenment into the broader framework of Western esotericism. This cross-cultural exchange could further enrich Rosicrucian teachings, creating a more universal and inclusive path to spiritual transformation.

As environmental concerns become increasingly urgent, Rosicrucianism's teachings about the interconnectedness of all life and the importance of living in harmony with nature may take on new relevance. The Rosicrucian tradition has always emphasized the importance of aligning oneself with the natural world as a way of understanding the divine order, and this principle can be applied to the modern environmental movement. By encouraging a deeper awareness of the spiritual dimensions of nature,

Rosicrucianism could contribute to a more holistic approach to environmental sustainability, one that recognizes the sacredness of the Earth and the need for humanity to live in balance with the planet's ecosystems. This ecological awareness could also lead to a revival of the ancient Rosicrucian practice of studying the healing properties of plants and natural remedies, fostering a renewed interest in holistic health practices that integrate physical, mental, and spiritual well-being.

In the realm of personal development, Rosicrucianism's focus on self-mastery, meditation, and inner transformation may continue to appeal to individuals seeking deeper meaning in their lives. As modern society becomes increasingly fast-paced and materialistic, many people are turning to spiritual practices as a way of finding balance, peace, and purpose. Rosicrucianism's teachings about the importance of meditation, contemplation, and self-reflection are well-suited to address these needs, offering a structured path to self-realization and spiritual growth. In the future, Rosicrucian practices may become even more accessible through the use of technology, with online meditation courses, virtual communities, and digital libraries allowing individuals from around the world to connect with Rosicrucian teachings and traditions.

The role of symbolism, ritual, and sacred geometry in Rosicrucianism may also continue to evolve in the future. These elements have always been central to the tradition, serving as tools for meditation, spiritual insight, and initiation. As modern art and architecture increasingly explore the use of sacred geometry and symbolic language, Rosicrucianism's emphasis on the hidden meanings behind shapes, symbols, and forms could inspire new artistic and architectural movements. The use of sacred geometry in urban planning, architecture, and design may become a way to create spaces that promote spiritual harmony and well-being, reflecting the Rosicrucian belief that the material world is a reflection of divine order.

Rosicrucianism's emphasis on community and the concept of the "invisible college" may also find new expressions in the future. As people seek deeper connections and shared spiritual experiences, Rosicrucian groups and study circles may expand both in-person and online, creating global networks of individuals dedicated to the pursuit of wisdom and spiritual growth. These communities could serve as modern iterations of the ancient Rosicrucian brotherhood, where seekers of truth come together to support each other on the path to enlightenment and to work for the betterment of humanity.

Conclusion

In conclusion, this collection, *Rosicrucianism: Esoteric Tradition, Philosophy, and Legacy of the Rosicrucian Order*, provides an in-depth exploration of the mysticism, symbols, philosophy, and enduring influence of the Rosicrucian tradition. Across these four volumes, readers have journeyed through the origins of the Rosicrucian brotherhood, delving into the ancient mysteries and spiritual ideals that have shaped its esoteric path. From the alchemical practices and symbols that define the inner work of transformation to the philosophical principles of the Rosy Cross that guide personal enlightenment, this bundle has illuminated the profound impact that Rosicrucianism has had on the Western esoteric tradition.

Book 1, *The Origins of Rosicrucian Mysticism: Secrets of the Ancient Brotherhood*, traces the early development of Rosicrucianism, offering insights into the brotherhood's mystical foundations and its deep connection to the currents of Hermeticism and Gnosticism. In Book 2, *Alchemy and the Rosicrucian Tradition: Unlocking the Hidden Symbols*, readers have explored the transformative power of alchemical symbolism, understanding how these sacred codes offer a blueprint for both material and spiritual refinement.

Book 3, *The Philosophy of the Rosy Cross: Enlightenment and Inner Transformation*, sheds light on the deeper philosophical underpinnings of Rosicrucian thought, revealing the path toward personal mastery, self-realization, and the inner alchemical process of enlightenment. Lastly, Book 4, *Rosicrucianism and Its Influence on Modern Occultism*, examines the enduring legacy of Rosicrucian ideals in contemporary spiritual movements, occult traditions, and modern magical practices, demonstrating how these ancient teachings continue to shape and inspire seekers of truth today.

This collection offers a comprehensive understanding of Rosicrucianism's profound role in shaping esoteric thought, presenting it as both a timeless tradition and a living, evolving philosophy. By bridging the spiritual wisdom of the past with the transformative practices of the present, Rosicrucianism remains a guiding light for those who seek inner awakening, self-transformation, and a deeper understanding of the hidden mysteries that govern the universe.

Milton Keynes UK
Ingram Content Group UK Ltd.
UKHW032032191024
449814UK00010B/597

9 781839 388729